The Mar...
Therapy ...

How does one obtain employment and succeed in the growing yet competitive field of family therapy? For anyone asking themselves this question, *The Marriage and Family Therapy Career Guide* is the resource to read. It is structured around a series of interviews with successful graduates of accredited MFT programs and covers a wide range of career options. Not only is up-to-date information on licensure and practice requirements for each state included, the authors also present agency, residential, coaching, medical, legal, tribal, academic, corporate, faith-based, and private practice options. The book ends with a section for those professionals who wish to practice abroad. This is an indispensable guide for marriage and family therapists wishing to start their career, or change their area of practice.

Anne Rambo, PhD, has taught in Nova Southeastern University's family therapy program for over 20 years and supervised hundreds of students who are now licensed marriage and family therapists (MFTs). She has developed an innovative program in the public schools helping to employ family therapists.

Tommie V. Boyd, PhD, is the chair of the family therapy department at Nova Southeastern University and is on faculty. She has over 30 years of clinical and supervision experience and is the recipient of an American Association for Marriage and Family Therapy (AAMFT) Leadership Award. She has developed programs helping to employ marriage and family therapists in medical settings, and was a key player in developing guidelines for marriage and family therapist employments in military settings.

Martha Gonzalez Marquez, PhD, has been an educator, clinician, and supervisor for over 20 years. She has a thriving couples therapy practice and has mentored others into launching their own practices in diverse settings. She is passionate about issues of ethics, inclusion, social justice, and supervision and has written and presented on these topics both nationally and internationally.

The Marriage and Family Therapy Career Guide

Doing Well While Doing Good

Anne Rambo, Tommie V. Boyd, and Martha Gonzalez Marquez

Routledge
Taylor & Francis Group

NEW YORK AND LONDON

First published 2016
by Routledge
711 Third Avenue, New York, NY 10017

and by Routledge
2 Park Square, Milton Park, Abingdon, Oxon, OX14 4RN

Routledge is an imprint of the Taylor & Francis Group, an informa business

Library of Congress Cataloging in Publication Data
Names: Rambo, Anne Hearon, author. | Boyd, Tommie V. |
Marquez, Martha Gonzalez.
Title: The marriage and family therapy career guide: doing well while doing
good/Anne Rambo, Tommie V. Boyd, and Martha Gonzalez Marquez.
Description: New York, NY: Routledge, 2016.
Includes bibliographical references and index.
Identifiers: LCCN 2015038716| ISBN 9781138853058 (hbk: alk. paper) |
ISBN 9781138853065 (pbk: alk. paper) | ISBN 9781315723044 (ebk)
Subjects: LCSH: Family psychotherapy. | Family psychotherapy—Practice.
Classification: LCC RC488.5 R353 2016 | DDC 616.89/156—dc23
LC record available at http://lccn.loc.gov/2015038716

ISBN: 978-1-138-85305-8 (hbk)
ISBN: 978-1-138-85306-5 (pbk)
ISBN: 978-1-315-72304-4 (ebk)

Typeset in Perpetua and Bell Gothic
by Florence Production Ltd, Stoodleigh, Devon, UK

Contents

1   Introduction: About This Book and About Marriage and Family Therapy   1
    Anne Rambo, Tommie V. Boyd, and Martha Gonzalez Marquez

2   Inclusivity in MFT: Working Across and Within Borders   7
    Christine Ajayi Beliard, Josiane Bonte Apollon, and Daniel Mendel

SUCCESS STORIES   **11**

3   About Private Nonprofit Agencies   13
    Anne Rambo

    Our Success Stories Recommend . . .   *14*
    Andrea's Story   *14*
    Fabiola's Story   *17*
    Trahern's Story   *19*
    Neolita's Story   *20*
    Liz's Story   *22*

4   About Residential Treatment Settings   25
    Tommie V. Boyd

    Our Success Stories Recommend . . .   *25*
    Jamie's Story   *26*
    Nancy's Story   *28*
    Lisa's Story   *29*
    Sara's Story   *31*

5   About Private Practice Settings   35
    Martha Gonzalez Marquez

    Our Success Stories Recommend . . .   *35*
    Idit's and Alina's Story   *36*
    Alonso's Story   *38*

Julien's Story   *41*
Tequilla's Story   *42*
Katie's Story   *44*

6   **About School-Based Settings**   47
Anne Rambo

Our Success Stories Recommend . . .   *47*
Philip's Story   *48*
Walter's Story   *49*
Susy's Story   *51*
Farheen's Story   *53*

7   **About Collaborative Settings with Other Professions
(Medicine and Law)**   55
Tommie V. Boyd

Our Success Stories Recommend . . .   *55*
Brian's Story   *56*
Randy's Story   *57*

8   **About Coaching**   61
Martha Gonzalez Marquez

Our Success Stories Recommend . . .   *62*
Alex's Story   *62*
Gaby's Story   *63*
Katia's Story   *65*
Trish's Story   *67*

9   **About Military Settings**   71
Anne Rambo

Our success Stories Recommend . . .   *71*
Anthony's Story   *72*
Laura's Story   *74*
Elissa's Story   *76*
Ronella's Story   *78*
Michele's Story   *81*

10   **About Managed Care Settings**   83
Tommie V. Boyd

Our Success Stories Recommend . . .   *83*
Anne-Marie's Story   *84*

Shazia's Story *85*
Fariha's Story *88*

11 **About University and Postgraduate Settings**   **91**
Martha Gonzalez Marquez

Our Success Stories Recommend . . . *91*
Rosario's Story *92*
Ili's Story *93*
Jacquie's Story *96*

12 **About Faith-Based Settings**   **99**
Anne Rambo

Our Success Stories Recommend . . . *99*
Patti's Story *100*
Leslie's Story *101*
Simone's Story *103*
Bobbi's Story *104*
Amnah's Story *106*

13 **About Indian Health Services and Related Settings**   **109**
Tommie V. Boyd

Our Success Stories Recommend . . . *109*
Bryan's Story *110*
Holly's Story *111*
Samantha's Story *113*

14 **About Corporate Settings and Entrepreneurial Work**   **117**
Martha Gonzalez Marquez

Our Success Stories Recommend . . . *117*
Marilyn's Story *118*
Jodi's Story *119*
Avi's Story *122*

15 **About Equine-Assisted Family Therapy**   **125**
Anne Rambo

Our Success Story Recommends . . . *125*
Talia's Story *125*

16 **About International Settings**   **129**
Tommie V. Boyd

Our Success Stories Recommend . . . *129*

Karen's Story   *129*
Doreen's Story   *130*
Jonathan's Story   *130*
Pei-Fen's Story   *131*

17   And in Conclusion . . .   133
Anne Rambo, Tommie V. Boyd, and Martha Gonzalez Marquez

Index   135

Chapter 1

Introduction

About This Book and About Marriage and Family Therapy

Anne Rambo, Tommie V. Boyd, and Martha Gonzalez Marquez

WHO WE ARE

This book is designed for marriage and family therapists at the beginning of their careers, or those interested in career growth and mobility. The three primary authors are long-term marriage and family therapy educators who have watched graduates go out into the world for over 25 years, and marveled at the varieties of positive outcomes. We have interviewed 53 marriage and family therapists who are successful in their chosen work settings, and identified what makes for success in each setting. Our interview subjects are listed in each section. While the three of us (Rambo, Boyd, and Marquez) collaborated on all interviews and on the book itself, each of us took primary responsibility for specific work-setting sections. Our names are listed under that setting along with those we interviewed, who are co-authors for their personal stories. All of our interviewees—our success story examples!—have master's degrees in family therapy. Unless otherwise specified, that master's degree is from a COAMFTE (Commission on Accreditation in Marital and Family Therapy Education) accredited program in the United States. While some of our subjects have additional degrees or certifications, our focus will be on what they can do with their master's in marriage and family therapy. "Marriage and family therapy" is the accepted legal name for our field, and includes services provided to both gay and straight couples, unmarried couples, individuals, and groups, as well as families. And that brings us to our discussion of the unique aspects of marriage and family therapy.

ABOUT THE FIELD OF MARRIAGE AND FAMILY THERAPY

Marriage and family therapy represents a relational way of looking at the world; a commitment to relational values; and also a profession, with its own distinct identity and credentialing. It is a comparatively young profession, originating in the 1950s and only recently accepted in all states of the United States and most countries. This relative newness at times challenges marriage and family therapists to work harder to explain their professional identity than those with more familiar designations such as psychologists and psychiatrists may have to do. Yet this newness has also meant marriage and family therapists have been free to move into a wide range of career options, and have ever-widening possibilities before them. The Bureau of Labor Statistics estimates marriage and family therapy as a field will grow by 30.6 percent a year, a faster rate than other mental health professions.

ABOUT THIS BOOK

In this chapter, we will briefly discuss the unique ideas of marriage and family therapy, the relational values, and the path to professional licensure. We will offer tips and techniques for identifying the areas of specialization within the field that will fit best for you. In the next chapter, we will take a look at the increasingly inclusive and diverse community of marriage and family therapists.

Then we move into our success story examples! We will consider how marriage and family therapists get jobs, and in what practice areas, and give examples of successful marriage and family therapists in each type of setting. These case examples are not meant as blueprints to copy, but as stories to inspire. They are to help you, the reader, get started on your own professional journey, and become aware of the wide range of possibilities open to you. Finally, we will conclude with general recommendations for success in this field, gleaned from our own experiences and from those of our success examples.

WHAT'S SO SPECIAL ABOUT MARRIAGE AND FAMILY THERAPISTS?

Marriage and family therapists do not necessarily see whole families; they may see individuals, couples, or groups. The professional title refers to marriage, but this includes all types of couples, whether legally married, straight or gay, divorced/remarried, or in any combination of circumstances. What makes marriage and family therapy distinct is its relational focus. An example may help to make this clear. Let us consider a woman in her 30s complaining of feeling sad and overwhelmed, shortly after the birth of her first child. Other mental health professions would consider her biological state, including possible postpartum depression, and her individual thinking processes, which could also be contributing to depressive thinking. A marriage and family therapist would consider these factors also. But a marriage and family therapist would also consider context: Who is helping her raise this child? What changes has becoming a mother made in her other relationships, including her relationship with her own parents? How supported does she feel by family, friends, and possible employer? These are all important considerations as well. Marriage and family therapy is highly effective and often brief, compared to other models of therapy, because all of these factors are taken into account.

Marriage and family therapy models are derived from a variety of underlying systemic theories. The oldest of these is general systems theory. Ludwig von Bertanlanffy is generally considered the originator of general systems theory. Von Bertanlanffy was a biologist, and his ideas stem from the consideration of living systems. While he began work on the theory in the mid-1920s, he began publishing in the area in the 1930s. The ideas of general systems theory, now widely accepted in the field, include that the whole is greater than the sum of the parts; that systems can usefully be viewed in terms of hierarchy, executive organization, and subsystems; and that the system itself strives towards preservation, so that individual members of the system can be considered to act in the service of the system as well as in their own interests. These ideas have informed or influenced all models of family therapy.

Couples therapy and some models of family therapy have been heavily influenced by attachment theory, which came next in time, developed in the 1940s. The focus of attachment theory is the mother/child unit as a relationship, rather than on the individual psyche of either one alone, and this relational focus has been continued in the field of object relations. Attachment theory and object relations remain an influence on some models of family therapy and have also been an influence on specific models of couple therapy.

Next in time we come to natural systems theory. Murray Bowen is considered the originator of natural systems theory. Bowen was a psychoanalytically trained psychiatrist who became a family therapist, and this theory dates from the 1950s. Bowen proposes that all life proceeds from less differentiation towards more differentiation. This can be seen at the level of cells, and at the level of nation states. Within the family, however, it is seen in the growth of the child from a symbiotic state to a more mature, differentiated relationship with the family of origin. Those models most influenced by natural systems theory are the intergenerational models of family therapy.

Also in the 1950s, cybernetic ideas about systems were introduced. Cybernetics is the comparative study of intelligences, and Norbert Weiner, involved in the development of computers, is generally given the credit for inventing cybernetics. However, Gregory Bateson contributed his own unique perspective to these ideas, blending cybernetic ideas about communication and pattern with his background as an anthropologist. Bateson contributed the ideas of nonpathologizing, circular causality (that human interactions arise out of complex circular feedback loops, for which no one person is responsible), multiple realities (that everyone sees the world differently, and this should be respected), and an ecological sensitivity to intervention, leading those therapists who practice from a Batesonian perspective to avoid normative ideas about families and focus on minimalist interventions. This emphasis on relationship has influenced all models of family therapy, but in particular the brief and postmodern models.

Michel Foucault was a French philosopher writing in the 1960s. His work has affected the field of family therapy primarily through the influence of Michael White, an originating narrative family therapist. White took Foucault's ideas about privileged vs. submerged voices, and socially constructed personal narratives, to craft a therapy which helped to free clients from socially imposed limits on their views of self. Narrative therapy has focused on issues of power and privilege and the therapist's self. Finally, imposed limits on their views of self has influenced all models of family therapy, in particular the brief and postmodern models, as a field, but most directly on narrative therapy models. Feminist critiques of family therapy worldwide have brought about an additional wave of questioning of power and privilege within relationships, especially along gender lines.

Suggested additional reading is given at the end of this chapter on the different models of family therapy, and the history behind each one. For now, the central point we wish to make is simply that it is the focus on relationship and context that makes marriage and family therapy unique.

HOW TO BECOME A MARRIAGE AND FAMILY THERAPIST

At first, when these new ideas about systems were beginning to take hold, mental health professionals who were already qualified as psychologists, psychiatrists, and social workers redefined themselves as family therapists as they became familiar with these relational ideas. Over time, however, a younger generation of potential therapists wanted to learn from the beginning to think in relational and contextual terms. At present, there are about 50,000 marriage and family therapists in the United States and Canada. While only 11 states recognized marriage and family therapists as a distinct profession in 1986, by 2009 all 50 states in the US (and the District of Columbia) licensed marriage and family therapists. Two provinces in Canada have followed suit. (See www.aamft.org for more information on professional recognition.)

Each state has its own unique licensing regulations. The website www.mft-license.com provides a useful overview of regulations in each state. There are considerable similarities, however. All states require a master's degree with particular specified coursework. COAMFTE accredited programs have an advantage in most states. After graduation with a master's degree, the beginning therapist will need to work under a clinical supervisor, either in private practice or in an agency setting, usually for the first two years after graduation (depending on the state). The beginning therapist will also have to take and pass a national licensing exam. The exam is given by the American Association of Marital and Family Therapy Regulatory Board (www.amftrb.org) but is administered through the state licensing board in each state. After obtaining the required supervised experience and passing the exam, the beginning therapist becomes a fully licensed marriage and family therapist, and can have an independent private practice if desired. Doctoral degrees in the field prepare the master's-level therapist for scholarship, teaching at the graduate level, and advanced clinical practice. Doctoral programs typically require that applicants already have a master's degree.

Federal loan programs provide some support during this training and licensure process. Graduate students are referred to http://studentaid.ed.gov for information on income-based loan repayment and public service loan forgiveness, for which qualified marriage and family therapists are eligible. The Indian Health Service and National Health Service Corps also provide loan forgiveness for licensed marriage and family therapists, in return for compensated employment with underserved populations. (See www.ihs.gov and www.nhsc.hrsa.gov for more detail.)

HOW TO BECOME THE BEST MARRIAGE AND FAMILY THERAPIST YOU CAN BE

The family therapist Bill O'Hanlon (www.billohanlon.com) identifies four questions to ask to help guide your career search:

1. What brings you **bliss?** What makes you most happy?
2. In what ways have you been **bless**ed? Do you have an influential mentor or opportunities that would guide you to a particular area of the field?
3. What makes you **piss**ed? Anger at injustice or inequity can be a powerful motivation.
4. And finally, in what areas have you been **diss**ed? Is there anyone whose lack of faith in you should be proved wrong?

These questions may help you identify areas of marriage and family therapy in which you would like to specialize.

Another tool to try is the ROPE exercise, developed by Rambo for use with at-risk youth to help set goals (Collins-Ricketts & Rambo, 2015). For the ROPE exercise, ask yourself:

R   is for **Recall**. Recall at least three times you felt you were successful at helping others and enjoying the process as well.

O   is for **Organize**. Organize those memories of times you felt you were successful at helping others and enjoyed the process as well.

For example, you may have positive memories of work with young children and their families.

P   is for **Present**, and moving into the future as well. Consider building on what has worked for you both in the *present* and future. Could you, for example, get more experience in preschool and early childhood settings now, perhaps as a volunteer or as part of an internship? Can you see yourself working in such a setting in the future?

E   is for **Expand**. Expand on your intentions, and tell other people about your interests. This is a great way to start networking!

SUCCESS STORIES

Subsequent sections of this book give examples of successful marriage and family therapists in private nonprofit agencies, residential treatment, and private practice settings, the most common contexts for practice. Then we move on to examine collaborative work with medical and legal professionals, and coaching, newer areas which are growing fast. Then we consider work with particular communities: the military, managed care organizations, university/postgraduate settings, faith-based practices, and work with Indian Health Services both in the United States and Canada. Finally we move to less usual but very promising areas of practice: corporate/entrepreneurial settings, and equine-assisted family therapy. Finally, we examine job opportunities internationally for graduates from COAMFTE accredited master's programs. These success stories will give you specific ideas but also inspire you to identify what is unique about you as a marriage and family therapist, and, we hope, to pursue your dreams. Before moving to these success examples, we will consider inclusion, and the need for marriage and family therapists of both genders and all ethnic and cultural backgrounds.

RECOMMENDED READING

Rambo, A., West, C., Schooley, A., & Boyd, T. (Eds.) (2012). *Family therapy review: Contrasting contemporary models*. New York: Routledge.

Wetchler, J., & Hecker, L. (Eds.) (2014). *An introduction to marriage and family therapy* (2nd edn.). New York: Routledge.

Chapter 2

Inclusivity in MFT

WORKING ACROSS AND WITHIN BORDERS

Christine Ajayi Beliard, Josiane Bonte Apollon, and Daniel Mendel

DIVERSITY AND INCLUSIVITY IN MARRIAGE AND FAMILY THERAPY

The field of marriage and family therapy is one of great attraction to not only potential clients, but also prospective clinicians. The paradigmatic view of change and the systemic focus is captivating. Oftentimes what remain invisible are the demographic and contextual factors—some that haunt our field, and others that are to be celebrated. It is only fair that those interested in a potential or continuing career in the field of MFT are aware of the diversity and inclusivity concerns of our field. In 2002, a report was published in *Family Therapy* magazine (Manderscheid et al., 2002). Although this was 12 years ago, it is one of the most recent breakdowns of demographic variables for MFTs. In this report, it was shared that "the mean age of MFTs is 54, 60% are women, and they are predominantly European American, 91%. African American, Hispanics, Native Americans, Asians and 'others' represent 3%, 2.1%, 1.5%, 1.4%, and 2.2% respectively." Although less than 10 percent of MFTs are of color, over half of client families are ethnic minorities. This speaks to the racial disparity in recruiting and retaining MFTs of color (Hernández, Taylor, & McDowell, 2009).

It is also important to note that 12 years ago the average age of MFTs was 54. The aging of family therapists is no secret. Although this may appear to be a problem, it also opens up many doors for younger clinicians. A large proportion of MFTs are entering the retirement phase of their careers, leaving administrative, training, research, faculty, and clinical jobs available to those more recent to the field. This is definitely something to celebrate for those beginning their professional career as a marriage and family therapist.

GENDER AND MARRIAGE AND FAMILY THERAPY

Over the past 12 years, the gender makeup of our training programs has further shifted. According to the American Association of Marriage and Family Therapy, 84.6 percent of students enrolled in accredited MFT programs identify as female (Program Demographic Data, 2014). Women are entering the field at extraordinary rates. Although this is to be celebrated, the undergirding issues of power and privilege cannot be separated from this trend. As women flock to the field, issues of gender–wage disparity persist, with male therapists earning more than their female counterparts. Interestingly, this is not unique to family therapy, as the trend of pay is often connected to the gender makeup of a field. This should push us all to recognize and hold accountable employers of family therapists. Beyond this, gender processes within and beyond our training programs and practice settings must stay at the forefront of our work.

We live in a time when the awareness of the fluidity between genders is increasing. While this is to be celebrated, it does not mean we should shy away from recognizing the differences in gender that remain present biologically, developmentally, and that still dominate the current cultural discourse. As family therapists we observe, interact, and impact a wide variety of systems. Recognizing the intricacies and influences gender has on any given system is crucial to the MFT field.

Finding your place in the field of family therapy is inextricably tied to understanding the influence of gender. What happens to male privilege when masculinity is lacking on the front lines of our field? How does being a man or woman shape one's clinical lens? In what ways does one's gender role support clients, and in what ways might it hinder the work? Are there areas to be explored in the family therapy field where maleness could help bridge gaps? These questions, and many more, have been at the forefront for clinicians, faculty, students, administrators, and organizations, as being male now means being under-represented in the field of family therapy.

It is not uncommon for clients to request a male therapist. This phenomenon makes sense in the construct of a profession and environment that is mostly comprised of women. What a male therapist may do might be similar to that of their female colleagues; however, a male presence in the therapeutic system provides gender diversity and opportunities that some clients want and need. This is something that must be acknowledged and further explored.

Sexual orientation and transgender issues must also be considered in our training and work as family therapists. Marriage and family therapists are often sought out by organizations and agencies to work with sexual minorities and their families, as our systemic understanding and nonpathologizing stance helps to empower clients, colleagues, and larger systems. Advocacy and protest has led to social reform in our country. MFTs have a responsibility to be accessible and provide relevant services to LGBTQ clients and their families. The intersectionality of race, ethnicity, gender, and sexuality is vital in our conceptualization of responsive care.

GLOBAL REACH OF MFTS WORKING ACROSS AND WITHIN BORDERS

Marriage and family therapy's reach is constantly expanding. It is critical that a global perspective be embraced. Technology, globalization, and migration have mandated an international understanding of relationships. American ethnocentrism, or the privileging of Western ideas and practices, is still apparent in our field, but this is beginning to be challenged by our clients and demographic shifts in our society.

The Knowledge Age gave birth to globalization and massive socioeconomic, political and technological changes across the world (Wieling & Mittal, 2002). Family systems worldwide are challenged by complex changes in family structures, "making them specialists in a world of specialists" (Ng, 2003, p.4). By contrast, marriage and family therapists (MFTs) have unexploited their multisystemic orientation to meet the rapid demands of global mental health, limiting their engagement with the broader parts of the population in the US and abroad (Wieling & Mittal, 2002).

Subsequently, Wieling and Mittal (2002) emphasize how the complexity of human dilemmas worldwide may compel family therapist academicians and practitioners to try "to save the planet" with another clinical model or theory. Instead they may opt to adopt a firm commitment to integrate in their approach to ethnic, gender, and cultural borderland issues what we call a global, collective, systemic consciousness. A perception of the MFT role connected to a bigger picture than our "little, petty selves" (O'Hanlon, 2015, p. 11).

Globalization challenges us to sustain interconnectedness, multiplicity, plurality, and diversity in a fast-growing world (Ng, 2003). Yet Gergen (2009) posits that Western ideology of individualism not only de-emphasizes the connection between people and promulgates the idea of separation, but also foments isolation and distrust, preventing close intimate and committed relationships with others.

For many, the choice of being agents of change, "bearing the torch", in foreign lands may appear difficult. Clear are the challenges and "growing pains" to develop and establish systemic family therapy around the globe (Ng, 2003). Different languages, cultures, and landscapes may be anxiety provoking. Yet our imagination can move us from being outsiders to insiders, finding new opportunities for all involved (Wright & Flemons, 2002).

Thus, our training in systems thinking allows future and seasoned family therapists to connect with worldwide families and organizations and bring about global change, working in multidisciplinary sectors and geographies. From

9

expanding our systemic field to the rest of the world, new family therapy practitioners can cross and enter borders, creating meaningful connections and intimate relationships in global wholeness.

There are myriad social factors and dimensions that must be considered, including but not limited to race, ethnicity, nationality, gender, sexuality, ability, body composition, health, region, socioeconomic status, and culture. The beauty of family therapy is that our theories, models, and epistemology allows for us to consider and be responsive to the contextual factors that can be so vital to our work. It is our hope the field of family therapy is able to not only become more sensitive to the influence of contextual variables, but to become more intentional and responsive in our work.

REFERENCES

Collins-Ricketts, J., & Rambo, A. (2015). The Promise program. *International Journal of Solution Focused Practices, 3*(2), available online at www.ijsfp.com.

Gergen, K. (2009). *An invitation to social construction* (2nd edn.). New York: SAGE Publications Ltd.

Hernández, P., Taylor, B. A., & McDowell, T. (2009). Listening to ethnic minority AAMFT approved supervisors: Reflections on their experiences as supervisees. *Journal of Systemic Therapies, 28*(1), 88–100.

Manderscheid, R. W., Brown, D. Y., Milazzo-Sayre, L. J., & Henderson, M. J. (2002, March/April). Crossing the quality chasm of racial disparities. *Family Therapy Magazine, 1*(2), 14–17.

Ng, K. S. (2003). *Global perspectives in family therapy: Development, practice, trends.* New York: Routledge.

O'Hanlon, B. (2015). *Solution-oriented spirituality: Connection, wholeness, and possibility for therapist and client.* New York: W. W. Norton.

Program Demographic Data (2014). Retrieved August 6, 2015, from www.aamft.org/iMIS15/AAMFT/Content/COAMFTE/Program_Demographic_Data.aspx.

Wieling, E., & Mittal, M. (2002). Expanding the horizons of marriage and family therapists. *Journal of Feminist Family Therapy, 14*(1) 53–62.

Wright, K., & Flemons, D. (2002). Dying to know: Qualitative research with terminally ill persons and their families. *Death Studies, 26*(3), 255–271.

Success Stories

Chapter 3

About Private Nonprofit Agencies

Anne Rambo

This is a common setting for entry-level positions for new graduates in marriage and family therapy. Agencies of this type offer mental health services to a low-income population, and receive funding through Medicaid and other government sources and from private donations as well. They may also receive funding from school district and from law enforcement agencies interested in prevention, and may accept private pay as well from clients able to pay for services. Typically, at-risk youth and their families are the target population. Family therapists working with such agencies often offer community-based therapy, meaning they meet with the targeted clients and their families at their homes, in schools, and in community-based settings, not just in an office setting. Such family therapy intervention is evidence based and highly effective with at-risk youth, as determined by the federal government (www.crimesolutions.gov).

Some agencies allow the therapist to determine the model, as long as it is effective; others require fidelity to an evidence-based model, with national oversight and supervision. (For evidence-based jobs nationwide, check out www.mstjobs.com.) In either case, this type of work provides much experience for beginning therapists, and hours towards licensure. At any given time, agencies such as this tend to be hiring for marriage and family therapists. Salaries can be on the low side for the profession—typically, from $30,000 to $42,000 annually, depending on the part of the country. Entry-level positions may be a bridge to licensure and eventual private practice. Many of those interviewed for this book, who are now in other settings, started out their careers as community-based family therapists for private nonprofit agencies.

But this setting should not be seen as just a starting place. Those committed to work in the private nonprofit sector who remain after licensure, and become clinical supervisors and clinical directors, are compensated at a higher salary—typically $45,000 to $60,000 annually, again depending in part on location. In addition, private nonprofit agencies offer opportunities to move into grant administration and interagency coordination.

In this section, we interview an entry-level marriage and family therapist working for a private nonprofit mental health agency (Andrea); her supervisor, who started at the same agency as an entry-level therapist (Fabiola); and a marriage and family therapist working for a grant-funded national evidence-based therapy program, administered through a local agency, but with fidelity to the national program (Trahern). We also interview two marriage and family therapists who started as therapists for private nonprofits, and became involved at the larger systems level—Neolita became a grant-funded program administrator, and Liz became a consultant coordinating multiple agencies.

OUR SUCCESS STORIES RECOMMEND . . .

Therapists who thrive on working for private nonprofit mental health agencies are flexible and good at time management, willing to put in time on weekends and evenings, but taking time off other times to avoid burning out. They maintain good humor and focus on the positives, even when every day may bring a different crisis or, as some like to call it, a new adventure. They do their paperwork together with their clients as much as possible to keep the process open and collaborative. This also minimizes time spent on paperwork when the client is absent, which can often not be billed for and which may become a burden to the therapist. Finally, therapists who do well working for private nonprofit agencies are comfortable working in community settings, and spend time getting to know their clients' neighborhoods. If you want to move up in the private nonprofit sector, get curious about the larger system issues—how is your program funded? Where do the grants and contracts come from? Looking into these issues can help you move to supervisor, program director, and consultant.

ANDREA'S STORY

Andrea Schneider, Entry-Level Agency Therapist

Background

Andrea graduated about two years ago with her master's in family therapy, from a COAMFTE accredited program. She chose an agency position to earn her required client contact hours for licensure, and to gain valuable experience. After obtaining licensure, which she hopes to have done soon, she plans to either move into a supervisory position or move into managed care.

What is this job like?

The agency Andrea works for receives referrals from child welfare, the public school system, the local law enforcement agency, and other private nonprofit agencies, as well as self-referrals from families seeking services. The program works with families who have at least one child between the ages of 0–18. A majority of the referrals involve child abuse, neglect, parenting and co-parenting concerns, and domestic violence. Andrea works with parents on learning new and different active-parenting skills, exploring their understanding of healthy and unhealthy relationships, and learning how to increase effective communication skills. She carries a caseload of between seven and eight families at one time and has the flexibility to create her own schedule around the convenience of the family. She meets with families at their homes and in community settings.

How do you get a job like this?

Andrea recommends looking for online job postings at sites such as www.indeed.com, and networking with others in the field. Job titles will typically be "family therapist," "child and family therapist," or "family counselor."

What is most rewarding?

Andrea says, "This may sound clichéd, but the most rewarding thing about my job is that for the most part, I actually feel like I am making a difference. Before going back to school for my master's in marriage and family therapy, I worked in the auto insurance industry for six years. There is a significant difference in overall job satisfaction because with this career, I believe I am helping people see themselves through a more positive perspective and, in turn, they are able to lead happier and more effective lives. Knowing that I played a role in that is incredibly rewarding. A 14-year-old client recently wrote a poem for me because she wanted me to know how much I helped her see who she really was and who she wanted to become. Parents have also thanked me for being able to connect with their children to the point where they saw significant positive changes in their child's attitudes and behavior." These kinds of intangible rewards keep family therapists going through the significant challenges of agency work.

What is most challenging?

Andrea reports finding a work/life balance is challenging, and this is a typical comment from entry-level agency family therapists. Andrea identifies one challenge is arranging and rearranging one's schedule so as to be available to families, perhaps on evenings or on weekends, and driving to homes. She says she can often be found hanging around in neighborhood coffee shops, working on case notes while waiting to see her next client. Successful agency family therapists organize their schedules to allow time for themselves and their own families, while remaining flexible and understanding this is not a 9-to-5 type of job.

15

What about your MFT training is most helpful to you?

Andrea builds every day on the concepts of systems thinking. As she describes, "I try to engage as many members of the family as possible in order to gather as many perspectives to be able to gain greater insight into what is actually going on in the family. I have had many parents tell me that they want me to 'fix' their child and get them to behave better. I use that opportunity to explain that their engagement and participation in family therapy is essential in helping me work with their child because the parents are the experts in their own life and in their child's life; I am there as a guide to help facilitate the changes they would like to occur. For the most part, the families appreciate that I want their input and thoughts, the foundation of systems thinking. Considering all the systems involved can further success, rather than just focusing on the identified client with the 'problem.'" Andrea also notes she learned in her graduate program the importance of self-care and of having a strong support system of colleagues in the field. These are important tools in keeping one's balance in the rewarding, yet demanding, world of agency practice.

About diversity

Andrea was initially anxious about doing home visits, a required part of her job, as of most community-based private nonprofit agency jobs. She has some suggestions for other beginning therapists: "I try to be as warm and engaging as possible when I go to a home for the first time so that the family does not feel as though they need to be worried about the appearance of the house or if it will look bad if all the toys are not put away or there are dishes in the sink." She also follows basic safety guidelines: "I make sure that I feel safe where I am going and make sure that my supervisor and husband know where I am going in case of an emergency. Some of the neighborhoods and areas where my families live are not the safest, but after doing this for almost two years, I have developed more comfort with all different neighborhoods. Once there is a trust and rapport built with the family, they will typically look out for me, and walk me to my car if they know that it would be better for me to be seen with them rather than going out alone." As a young white Jewish woman, Andrea has found home and community visits to be invaluable in helping her work with diverse clients. "Working in South Florida, I am constantly working with a variety of populations from different countries, ethnicities, and religions. Over time, having sessions in the home rather than in an office setting allows me to get a more realistic picture of the family dynamics in the home. I saw clients at an office during my internship while in school, and, in comparison, I feel I am able to gain greater insight into the family and their problems and strengths at their home where the family is in their natural environment, rather than taking the family out of their comfort zone and putting them into an office setting."

FABIOLA'S STORY

Fabiola Gutierrez, Clinical Supervisor

Background

Fabiola is the Program Director for the Family Skill Builders program for a private nonprofit agency. She is also a clinical supervisor and is our interview subject Andrea's supervisor. In addition to her master's in family therapy, Fabiola is a Certified Trainer and Facilitator for Active Parenting Now and a Certified Trainer for Batterers Intervention Program.

What is this job like?

Fabiola notes: "I am responsible for the direct supervision of staff as well as insuring programmatic goals, objectives and agency policy and procedures are met. I work as a liaison with the community, sister agencies in child welfare, legal, educational and mental health and juvenile court/dependency court systems, the family, funders, and I serve on community-based associations. On a daily basis, I provide supervision of the intake and screening process for children, their families, and volunteers. I work closely toward program growth and expansion with the Project Administrator. I provide clinical supervision to therapists and interns weekly. I conduct team meetings and peer reviews twice per month. I provide training in parenting and co-parenting curriculums. And, in addition, I assist therapists providing co-therapy and supervision during home visits." The program works because of Fabiola's hands-on approach.

How do you get a job like this?

Fabiola was an in-home family therapist herself for this agency for two years, and was promoted upon becoming licensed. She had past experience as a parent educator and parenting program director for a private practice. She credits her master's internship, with autistic children and their families, as having developed her love for work with families. She notes, "This internship was a most meaningful and rewarding experience I hold very close to my heart. I learned through these wonderful autistic children and their families composed of parents, grandparents, and siblings, compassion, strength, courage, dedication, vision like no other. I believe this was the foundation of my MFT work in the community." Fabiola recommends, "Develop professional mentoring relationships at every step in your professional journey."

What is most rewarding?

Fabiola finds it most rewarding to help families meet their goals. Her agency also supervises master's-level interns in their practicum experience, and hires many recent graduates: "I also love mentoring MFT interns, teaching, and sharing my experiences from graduate school until now."

What is most challenging?

Some of the biggest challenges Fabiola identifies "are working with undocumented families, families with eviction notices, and families with extreme economic hardship. Our program utilizes flex funds and value-added funds for emergency situations only. However, each family's needs are different. The Family Skill Builders team works very hard to provide crisis intervention and community resources, including informal supports." It is always difficult when resources are lacking, as is the case for many of the populations served.

What about your MFT training is most helpful to you?

For Fabiola, "Systemic thinking and respect for diversity have been the essential values of my work as a Program Director." She has made it a point to hire bilingual therapists and case managers, and to work within the communities of greatest need.

About diversity

This is a topic Fabiola has given much thought and consideration. She explains, "I was born in Lima, Peru; I am a US citizen. I am female, Hispanic, and of heterosexual orientation. I have been a co-parent for 14 years and have gained great insight in co-parenting skills personally and professionally. I understand the difficulties of a divorce and how it directly affects the children involved. In addition, I am able to utilize my personal experiences from a parent perspective and a child perspective: through my daughter's experiences of living in two households, separation in holidays, feeling invisible loyalties, feeling at a loss as to my experience as a parent, making sure her needs are met, and she is able to survive and thrive in this society. Involving both parties and working as a partnership has been extraordinary work on a personal level and professionally. At the same time, I am able to provide the support needed for biological parents and step-parents through parenting and co-parenting sessions." Thus, for Fabiola the personal and professional come together.

TRAHERN'S STORY

*Trahern LaFavor, National Evidence-Based Program
Clinical Supervisor*

Background

Trahern is a clinical supervisor for a national evidence-based family therapy program, administered through a local nonprofit agency. His program works with delinquent and at-risk youth. He also has a private practice on the side.

What is this job like for you?

Trahern conducts weekly individual, group, and team supervision. He assures clinical documentation is consistent with grant and agency requirements. Trahern also provides supportive and corrective feedback to clinicians to promote client outcomes. He provides direct clinical training to assure competency in all clinical areas relating to their implementation of the evidence-based model. He also reviews all assessments for completeness and fidelity to the model.

How do you get a job like this?

Trahern has been a supervisor in this same program for two agencies now. Prior to that time, he worked at the clinician level for the same program for four years, and after receiving awards for his clinical skills, and licensure, he was promoted to supervisor. He has had extensive training in the evidence-based model, provided whilst he worked for the national program.

What is most rewarding?

Trahern comments: "The most rewarding aspect of my job is providing super-vision to staff—helping them successfully adhere to the principles of the evidence-based model to treat at-risk youth. It's also rewarding to work with other professionals such as social workers, mental health counselors, psychiatrists, and other community providers. My background in systems theory affords me the opportunity to collaborate with multiple disciplines."

What is most challenging?

It can be difficult to train new clinicians to both acquire and maintain fidelity to the model. The terms of the grant funding require commitment to this particular model. This can be a challenge, but Trahern finds that with continuing supervision, clinicians new to the model and the program can adjust.

19

What about your MFT training is most helpful to you?

Trahern identifies systems thinking as critical to collaborating with multiple professionals, and larger systems. He also utilizes a solution-focused approach in his supervision as well as in his therapy.

About diversity

As an African-American man, married, and the father of two sons, Trahern appreciates the importance of strong families. It is meaningful to him to work with an evidence-based model with a proven track record of strengthening families and preventing young people from falling into the criminal justice system.

NEOLITA'S STORY

Neolita,* Grant Management/Administration

Background

Neolita is the Director of Program Development for a large private nonprofit agency. In this capacity, she is responsible for administrating over 4.2 million dollars in grant-funded projects. She also supervises and trains staff.

What is this job like?

This is a "big picture" job, which requires Neolita to use her abilities to analyze systems. Often, Neolita will identify a need, coordinate resources from her own and other agencies to address that need, explore with management about program needs and possible funding opportunities, and see the project through to completion. She is the pioneer of the College/Career Launch program. Neolita had identified that many of the young people with whom her organization works lacked a clear picture of options after high school. She coordinated with area colleges and universities and put together a program whereby youth were able to go on college tours, and learn about the application process.

How do you get a job like this?

Neolita worked for over 23 years for private nonprofit agencies. She was convinced that prevention is the preferred model because it addresses harmful behaviors in the early stages. As she notes, "So often, with my clients in jail, it all went back

* Last name has been withheld by request.

to childhood issues. There had to be a way to help people before they were victims of incarceration." She had past grant administration experience, and applied for a job as a grant coordinator at her current agency. At the time that seemed like a lateral move, or even a step down, but she knew she wanted to help children via prevention programs. The combination of her clinical experience and her grant experience has been dynamic, and she implements innovative and effective programs.

What is most rewarding?

Neolita describes "moments in time" when the impact of all her work becomes clear. One such moment came about during the College/Career Launch she organized. She looked over and saw "a young lady with a college backpack, a giveaway from one of the colleges, on her back. She was wearing it proudly. I knew she had never previously thought of herself as attending college. It's just a moment—when you can take a moment and say, 'Yeah, I did that. I was part of that.'" Such moments keep her going through a very busy schedule.

What is most challenging?

"Paperwork!" Neolita laughs. Grants and contracts require much documentation.

What about your MFT training is most helpful to you?

Neolita identifies systems training as critical in her work. She also credits the ability to "read" people and analyze interactions.

About diversity

Neolita notes, "As a person of color, and a woman, there have been times in the past when I did not feel valued or appreciated by supervisors, even though I was working very hard. I try to make a difference now in my supervision of younger staff." Neolita encourages and mentors, and sees her role as helping other younger staff to meet their goals. She works with staff trying to balance life/work issues, such as being a single mother and student. She believes that the success and wellbeing that we wish for the children that we serve must also be extended to our staff. The touching thankyou notes she receives from those she has helped in their professional journey are a testament to her efforts.

LIZ'S STORY

Liz Shulman, Clinical Consultant in Interagency Collaboration

Background

Liz is the Clinical Consultant for an interagency collaboration funded by her city government. This collaboration targets at-risk youth.

What is this job like?

Liz works with area agencies, schools, and juvenile probation to coordinate efforts. For example, in her city there was a recent upsurge in the number of teenage girls engaging in risky cutting behavior. Many of these girls knew each other, and at times the behavior was contagious. But the girls all attended different schools, and most were in treatment at different agencies. Liz brought together all the guidance counselors from the different schools involved and representatives from the various agencies, and brought in an outside consultant with expertise in this area to meet with them. This helped develop a focused, coordinated response. Liz also works extensively with Juvenile Review Boards in developing programs which offer alternatives to incarceration.

How do you get a job like this?

"Put yourself out there," Liz advises. Liz was working for a private nonprofit agency in the area of youth services. She was her agency's representative to an interagency collaborative review board. She volunteered and put in extra time, over and above what was required of her as an agency representative. When she left her agency to go into private practice, the city government officials who fund the interagency collaboration asked her if she would stay on part time, to coordinate between agencies. This part-time position led her to her current position.

What is most rewarding?

Liz identifies "building and enhancing relationships" as the most rewarding part of her work. She was also proud when her city was recently identified as a "model city" nationwide because of its collaborative approach to youth justice.

What is most challenging?

Self-care and time management are challenges for Liz, as she balances private practice with the increasingly busy work of interagency collaboration. She also mentions "barriers to information sharing", which occur when agencies are reluctant to divulge too much to other agencies, although this is changing.

What about your MFT training is most helpful to you?

Liz uses the concept of "restorative justice" in her work, and sees the relationship between this and narrative therapy, which she learned about in her MFT program. She feels she understands the restorative justice idea at a deeper level because of her MFT training. She also comments, "Context is huge," and she draws on systems thinking in all of her work.

About diversity

Liz found herself in the sometimes uncomfortable position of being a white woman from (compared to many of her juvenile clients) a relatively privileged background, working with low-income and minority clients and the community agencies that serve them. She has found it useful to understand the history behind a reluctance to trust, and works hard to "meet clients where they are." As her work in the community has become more known over time, she has had the happy experience of having former clients vouch for her to new clients. "I'll be referred a kid, and the kid will ask around, and someone will say, 'Oh, Liz? Liz from the North Shore? She's okay.' And that means a lot."

Chapter 4

About Residential Treatment Settings

Tommie V. Boyd

Residential treatment centers may be private nonprofits as well, but may be for-profit companies. They will typically address addictions and behavior that cannot be safely treated except with constant supervision. Generally they are insurance funded, although some may be private pay. The certification of choice for this setting is often a Certified Addictions Professional designation, as well as an MFT degree and possible licensure. MFTs will work as part of a treatment team in the residential program setting. Such settings can provide a feeling of intense camaraderie, and idyllic working conditions (if in a private, luxurious facility). However, it can also be very frustrating to work with clients who often relapse. Self-care is important. MFTs must also adjust to the fact that residential treatment and rehab facilities are big business and ethical standards can vary. We interviewed Jamie (a counselor in substance-abuse-related residential treatment settings), Nancy (the program director of a substance-abuse-related residential treatment program), Lisa (a therapist in an eating-disorder-related residential treatment program), and Sara (a clinical director for a homeless shelter).

OUR SUCCESS STORIES RECOMMEND . . .

Our interviewees recommend those working in residential settings maintain a high ethical standard, and set a standard for the field. Specialized training and credentials such as Certified Addictions Professional, in addition to family therapy training, may be useful. It is important to become prepared for this type of work—internship sites and specific experiences relevant to residential treatment center settings are vital. Nancy advises, "Don't go the easy route. I can't tell you how many times I have spoken to therapists early in their career that took an internship because it was a requirement and didn't research what they wanted to do in their career. Do your research! I spent over two months finding and then applying for my internship. They required I devoted 25 hours per week, which meant I had to give up my job at the time. However, I will tell you it was worth every moment and gave me enough knowledge to obtain my first job as a primary therapist." Jamie, Lisa, and Sara concur that experience in specialized treatment settings is vital. So is self-awareness, sensitivity to spiritual concerns, and one's own journey through the recovery process when indicated.

JAMIE'S STORY

Jamie Guerin, Therapist, Substance Abuse Agency

Background

Jamie is a Primary Therapist for a substance abuse treatment facility. He is a licensed marriage and family therapist, a Certified Addictions Professional, and a Certified Transgender Counselor. He also works in private practice and has a part-time job going into jails, seeing clients referred by the Department of Children and Families whose children have been placed in foster care due to their arrest under the influence.

What is this job like?

In the residential setting, in private practice, and in jail, Jamie sees many clients struggling with substance abuse, as well as couples (gay, straight, and transgender), and individuals arrested for DUI (driving under the influence). His advice for others wishing to work in this area, those graduating now, "would be to not be afraid of your skills and that above all else, you are healers and the world needs you." In the field of addiction, "Understand all approaches and the differences between 12-Step Recovery, therapy, harm reduction, faith-based support, the disease model, and recent advances in medicine including co-occurring disorders. Additionally, understand also the place of medications to help those in early recovery, as well as how the brain is affected by the use of substances."

How do you get a job like this?

Jamie worked as a bachelor's-level behavior technician in a residential setting while in graduate school. This helped with contacts in the field. He is also personally in recovery, which gave him additional credibility.

What is most rewarding?

Jamie notes, "The most rewarding part of my job is knowing that through my life experience and the skills I acquired in my MFT master's program, I can help others see that change is possible, available, and within them."

What is most challenging?

In common with many therapists, Jamie finds paperwork most challenging.

"The biggest challenges have been the paperwork as the treatment industry is governed by the insurance companies and monitored by the state agencies. As a therapist, it is a balance that must be made and at times is difficult to accomplish."

What about your MFT training is most helpful to you?

Jamie identifies specific models of family therapy which have been useful to him. "I use my marriage and family training utilizing the skills of three theories: solution focused, narrative, and strategic. Solution focused is essential in the recovery arena as clients need to focus on solutions in order to move past the devastation that substance abuse has made of their lives and their families. Narrative is utilized to help the client create a new story, as the story they have lived is one of self-defeating behavior. Strategic therapy is utilized to help the client see their addiction in a new light, as the disease of addiction is one of denial. As far as the skills that I have utilized in the field of addiction, the most important one is to be able to talk to all members of the family and work with them on the effects of substance abuse on the family and what they can do to help themselves and each other. A lot of the work by Minuchin and structural theory informs me."

About diversity

"As a recovering addict for over 28 years, I have a wealth of personal experience of recovery, relapse, therapy, meetings, marriage, divorce, single parenting, promotion to senior management, loss of job, loss of wealth, gain wealth, change of careers. So I believe I have a distinct advantage over someone who has not had those experiences. However, most of this country has some kind of contact with disease of addiction, someone in the nuclear or extended family. If you take a systemic relational view, then everyone is affected by the behavior of the person who uses substances. Specifically in the family, I look at boundaries, expectations, co-dependency, enabling, family history (Bowenian Theory) that inform me as a therapist of a pattern of behavior that a narrative approach can help make change in the recovering person and their families' lives.

"As a person who embraces the LGBT community, I am informed by my recent marriage (prior to Supreme Court ruling) to my wife, who is a talented award-winning chef who happens to be a transgender human being. This informs me through my empathy of others who have to live in this world with the last stereotype and discrimination of the 'T' in LGBT. As far as my own gender identity, I see myself on a continuum of male–female. Part of this is due to my almost 15 years of raising three children on my own without a woman (wife) in the home.

I have had to find parts of myself that were excluded because of my upbringing as white privileged male in the American society."

NANCY'S STORY

Nancy Spitzer, Program Director, Substance Abuse Treatment Center

Background

Nancy is Program Director at a substance abuse treatment center. She is the Program Director of the partial hospitalization program of a well-regarded in-patient chemical dual diagnosis treatment center. She rose to this position in less than five years after graduation.

How did you get this job?

I was recruited by a professional headhunter for the position and then interviewed with the company.

What is this job like?

It is Nancy's job to make sure the agency is adhering to all rules and regulations and to oversee the day-to-day operations of the program. She also supervises clinical staff, reviews documentation, and monitors all ancillary services.

How do you get a job like this?

Nancy was careful to select internship sites in the substance abuse area while she was working towards her master's degree. After graduation, she worked in substance abuse treatment centers. She was recruited for her current position. Her background before marriage and family therapy, in sales and public relations, has also helped her in this field.

What is most rewarding?

Nancy holds on to her belief that clients can change. As she comments, "It's difficult to explain on paper, but it is the moment that you can see a fierce determination in the client's eyes due to them being able to capture their own potential. I believe very much in empowering the individuals I work with and allowing them to be a part of the process. I feel I would be incapable as a therapist if I did not grow with my clients and give them the opportunity to see their own natural gifts."

What is the most challenging?

Most clients entering treatment centers have years of previous treatment that did not work for them. Working against discouragement and shame can be challenging.

What about your MFT training is most helpful to you?

Nancy reflects, "I think one of the main reasons I have been successful with clients in terms of connecting with them and seeing them grow into healthy, sober individuals is that I do not look at them directly as the 'problem.' I compare myself to a detective in terms of learning about all aspects of their lives to 'solve' the mystery or the barriers to recovery. I develop strong relationships with family members and attempt to start the groundwork for shifting the family dynamics along with helping my client become heard as a sober person. I try to understand what it is like to experience life as my client—culturally, mentally, physically, and spiritually."

About diversity

Nancy states, "I think it is hard to be a woman in this field and a woman that is not in sobriety. I was once told that men don't listen to me because they (male clients) can't be intimate with a 'young, pretty girl'. I took that feedback in for about two seconds, and then my entire body challenged that concept. I can acknowledge differences, but it doesn't mean that my gender limits my professional ability. I feel I have spent most of my time in my career proving my worth to a community that also wants to be accepted. I have spent time in supervision and with my colleagues developing my own voice as a therapist and now as a director. I always spend time working with female colleagues on allowing them to shine their light regardless of how others perceive them."

LISA'S STORY

Lisa Palmer, Eating Disorders, Inpatient/Intensive Outpatient Therapy

Background

Lisa is a licensed marriage and family therapist, with both a master's and a doctoral degree. She is also an AAMFT Approved Supervisor, certified as a hypnotherapist, and certified in Rapid Reduction Technique for the resolution of trauma. She is currently Clinical and Program Director of an intensive outpatient center she founded for the treatment of eating disorders, the Renew Center.

29

What is this job like?

Lisa's center provides "intensive customized therapy programs for eating disorders, trauma, addictions, and relationships." She also coordinates with other treatment providers.

How do you get a job like this?

Lisa worked in inpatient and residential facilities for eating disorders, and rose to the position of Clinical Director and Founder of an intensive outpatient eating disorder program at a hospital. She founded her own center so that people could get help while still living in their own homes; as she notes, "My approaches and style have proven effective for patients with tough to beat problems who might ordinarily require inpatient or residential programs."

What is most rewarding?

Lisa is emphatic about how rewarding results can be: "Seeing patients with tough to beat problems achieve results in relatively short periods of time usually within 60–90-day programs, and they go on to live successful, happy, healthy lives, without becoming permanent life patients." She has also seen her practice increase dramatically over time. She advises beginning therapists, "I can barely return all the calls I get, and patients book me for months at a time. But that came with a lot of very hard work and experience. You have to have something to offer and develop a track record of results. Put your time in, develop a program, and don't be afraid of setting up a business. Learn about marketing. Go on TV, radio, write articles, talk to people, be a role model in your own life. Too many therapists offer advice to patients, yet do not use it themselves. Believe in yourself, take care of yourself—practice what you preach. Figure out what you are really good at and develop a niche. Be your best self, and use all the tools and gifts you have been given to make a difference."

What is most challenging?

With her center increasingly busy, Lisa notes it can be challenging to make time for herself and keep a work/life balance.

What about your MFT training is most useful to you?

Lisa cites systemic thinking as critical. "The systemic training allows me to be able to approach a solution from a variety of angles and make better predictions about how certain interventions will unfold over time based on theories of change and the patient's nature and relationship system."

About diversity

This is an important topic for Lisa. "I'm half Dominican, half Italian American. My parents are immigrants with a hard work ethic and strong morals and values who represent the American dream. They have become successful with hard work and dedication over a period of time, and living honorably. They did not believe in psychiatry or counseling. I think this influenced me the most, because like other kids growing up, I too had bad things come up, but I learned how to best access and utilize strengths and resources I had within and around me without therapies or life coaching to overcome negativity and achieve possibilities. I think this nurtured a strong positive core belief system, good insight and judgment, and life skills. If I did find myself in turmoil, I had a solid base of belief in something better with an action plan to give me the best outcomes. As Italian-Dominicans, if we got angry, we forgave quickly. We believed in expressing ourselves and not holding anything in. My style makes patients very comfortable because it is a conversational style and even if they have nothing to say, or things get awkward in a heated family session, or they come in a hot mess, I handle things with confidence without letting emotions take over. I like patients to speak the truth. I always look for their sparkling moments and emphasize when that happens."

SARA'S STORY

Sara Smith, Supervisor, Behavioral Health Residential Homeless Shelters

Background

Sara has a master's degree in marriage and family therapy. She is also certified in advanced solution-focused therapy, advanced cognitive behavioral therapy, and other related trainings. She is the Supervisor of Behavioral Health for three related residential homeless shelters, and supervises interns from four different universities who work at these sites.

What is this job like?

Sara works with three other therapists, and 25 graduate interns, to provide mental health services to a diverse group of homeless individuals, many of whom are dually diagnosed with substance abuse and chronic mental health issues. As Sara describes it, "My responsibilities began immediately after any clients entering our program. I have to monitor all tasks and assign the team members on a daily basis. Each client will be interviewed upon arrival to our program and we have to complete an evaluation process, asking questions from the client in a formal face-to-face interview. These questions are carefully chosen to help the clinician plan to review the client's history of mental health and substance abuse issues, all the way to their current situation of becoming homeless. My number one responsibility is to remain nonjudgmental, join with the client and attempt to normalize the client's situation to the point that I gain their trust and they respond to the questions openly. This will ease the evaluation process more effectively. I then assess and diagnose the client according to the DSM 5, then choose a therapist to whom I can assign the client immediately. I monitor the assigned therapist's interaction with the client over time." Sara also works together with area hospitals, probation officers, judges, attorneys, and anyone else involved in a particular client's situation. She keeps outcome data on all clients as well. Choosing and supervising graduate interns also takes up time, but allows her to provide services for more clients.

How do you get a job like this?

Sara started out in the field doing in-home therapy for a private nonprofit agency, and subsequently worked for another agency as well. She learned a great deal from these positions, about assessment and working with the court system in particular, but was ready for a change when she applied to her present position. Her excellent assessment skills were key to her getting the job, but she has also expanded the job, once hired. As she tells, it, "Since I am a revolutionary, immediately after securing my position, I began to make constructive changes in the core of this department. I requested to have a bigger office and more pleasant environment for our clients to make them feel more welcomed to start their services. I began implementing all that I learned in regards to systemic thinking and diverse learning. I made certain that all charts are maintained according to the other agencies and everyone is respecting HIPAA rules in addition to the agency's rules. It was a difficult process since I had to satisfy two different supervisors. One supervisor was a psychologist who was opposed to MFT programs and every week had to inform me how much he disliked my school of therapy. Another supervisor was a recent graduate who was inexperienced. I used my systemic skills to balance their perspectives while holding on to my own. Six months later, I received an offer directly from the agency's president, to become a supervisor and manage both centers." This has now been expanded to cover three centers. Sara has increased the number of graduate interns from two to 25, greatly increasing the scope of services.

What is most rewarding?

Sara finds it rewarding to work with the homeless population, the "forgotten individuals" in our society. She also enjoys supervising and training graduate interns.

What is most challenging?

It is challenging that the homeless shelter program is limited to 60 days; Sara would wish for more time to work with clients who may have severe and long-standing problems.

What about your MFT training is most helpful to you?

Sara draws on a variety of models. "My work with the client starts with evaluating the client. Most of the questions at the evaluation stage come from solution-oriented, narrative thinking. That assists me with diagnosing and treatment planning. When the client reveals any mutigenerational issues regarding any sorts of abuse that runs in their family, I draw the Genogram and use the Bowenian Theory. For groups, I prepare materials related to psycho-educational, behavioral, structural, and cognitive behavioral therapy, that fits with the requirements of the agency." Sara also takes a systemic and collaborative approach in her supervision and with larger systems issues.

About diversity

Sara's experiences remind us that diversity can be an issue for our clients as well. Sara left Iran and lived in several European countries before coming to the United States; "Smith" is her married name. She comments, "Being Persian and coming from Iran actually assisted me to stand out in grad school. BUT, it was my biggest challenge at my work place and heart breaking dealing with a few of my clients.

Twice in the past I was asked by clients to leave their home when they found out I was Iranian. It broke my heart so severely. Some clients now are not familiar with my accent but they end up liking me possibly more because of my accent. I have also had difficulties with coworkers because of my accent. I always joke with them and tell them I am the only Sara Smith with an accent." Sara focuses on inclusion and diversity every day.

Chapter 5

About Private Practice Settings

Martha Gonzalez Marquez

Private practice settings are the goal for most graduates, and are the most common setting nationwide. To be in private practice, a marriage and family therapist must be either licensed, or under direct supervision by a qualified supervisor. Specifics vary depending on the state—look up the details at www.mft-license.com for your individual state. Salaries can range from six figures down to nothing—a therapist in private practice becomes an entrepreneur and small-business owner. Some private practitioners accept insurance, which often involves an application process in order to become accepted by an insurance panel; others utilize fee for service, accepting cash, checks, and credit cards, especially with services where insurance might be complex, for example with couples therapy. The freedom to practice independently is attractive to many marriage and family therapists: you are your own boss and, in part, limited only by the efforts you put in. You can design your own space; and you can choose your area of specialization. You can set your own hours and take time off as desired. However, it is important to consider challenges as well. As with any business, the therapist/owner will have to face competition and develop a sound business plan. We present interviews from Idit and Alina (recent graduates who went straight into private practice after graduation, under supervision); Alonso (who has a large private practice in an urban area, which employs other therapists as well); Julien (who is in private practice in a rural area); Tequilla (who runs her own private practice); and Katie (who has a solo private practice in an urban area, which focuses on supervision and training).

OUR SUCCESS STORIES RECOMMEND ...

Become a presence on social media—blog, post, and get your business out there on the Internet. In person, consider providing free workshops to the community, to advertise yourself and your services. A clearly identifiable specialty can help you set your practice apart from others, especially in a crowded urban area. Such specialties may include additional training in a model or with a particular population, but can also include life experiences such as speaking a second language or being part of a particular underserved community. Additional advice includes being creative, following your passion, becoming business savvy, developing goals, and practicing self-care. Julien and Katie both add that finding a *great* supervisor is very important. Tequilla advises networking is important, as is joining professional organizations in your area. Idit and Alina state, "There is no reason why a new graduate with a great clinical supervisor and some business-mind cannot make it out there."

IDIT'S AND ALINA'S STORY

Idit Sharoni and Alina Gershonov, MFT Registered Interns

Background

Idit and Alina are recent graduates, who practice under the supervision of a licensed colleague. Idit is the owner of Modern Family Therapeutic Solutions LLC. Alina is the owner of Inner Therapeutic Solutions, LLC. Both are in practice in Florida.

What is this job like?

Idit and Alina are both full time in private practice, working under the auspices of a licensed colleague until they become licensed. Idit sees couples and families, with a specialty in families struggling with school issues, based on her 18 years as a professional in the education system. Alina has significant experience with yoga and meditation and is also on the board of directors for a nonprofit yoga educational and healing organization; she specializes in personal growth, balance, and inspiration. Both Idit and Alina also talk with potential referral sources, write blogs, and offer workshops to the community. Both are also qualified hypnotherapists.

How do you get a job like this?

Idit had this vision from the beginning of her master's program. Alina did as well, commenting, "I always saw myself in a private practice setting; in fact I entered my master's program with the intention of going right into private practice after graduation." Both recommend finding the right clinical supervisor—one who understands the intricacies of private practice, and can advise on ethical and legal considerations as well as clinical. Finding the right colleagues for support and to associate with in practice is also important. Finally, it is crucial to understand the requirements for independent practice in your state. Alina adds, "One thing I do every day is BREATHE! Staying as mindful and present as possible is what I strive for on a daily basis. Self-care is beyond crucial in this field and yoga has been an absolute lifesaver for me. I do my best to stay active daily, whether it be yoga, the gym or a long walk; physical activity is key!"

What is most rewarding?

Idit sums it up nicely when she says, "After working for organizations for over 18 years of my life, I really enjoy the sense of being a business woman and making it on my own—a great sense of self-realization. This, of course, comes with a huge responsibility that is both financial and professional." Alina notes that "the most rewarding part of my job is when my clients' lives have been positively affected as a result of therapy. When I interned at the psychiatric hospital, most of the patients were in and out in a few days so I wasn't able to follow up or have any way of knowing if change occurred. Fortunately, now I am able to develop a therapeutic relationship with my clients and I am able to see the change that occurs. Knowing that I have made an impact and offered a helping hand into seeing new possibilities and hope for the future is what makes my job gratifying, to say the least." Both feel they have developed strengths in the areas of marketing and business planning, as well as clinical excellence.

What is most challenging?

It takes a time to build up a clientele. During this time, beginning therapists may need to work part time for an agency, or work with a more established practitioner as part of his or her therapy team. Marketing, setting fees, and becoming a business owner are not skills many therapists develop in their graduate programs; yet they will be essential for success in private practice.

What about your MFT training is most helpful to you?

Both cite systems thinking and respect for diversity as central to their work with clients. Idit notes, "My marriage and family training is the basis of everything that guides me through my journey as a therapist. In the therapy room I use models and ideas based on systems thinking, but not only then. Systems thinking has become part of who I am as a person. It is not a switch I can turn off and on. Therefore, it has guided my choices, from how I do therapy through how I vision my practice, to how I am as a professional, colleague, and person. One example is my ultimate vision of a holistic practice that comes from the notion that there may not be just one way to help people bring change into their lives. Another example is my work with families that is influenced by ideas such as context, reciprocity, interaction patterns, circularity, first- and second-order change, both/and approach, and more. Finding how a behavior makes sense in its context and keeping curiosity about my clients' experiences guide my work in every session regardless of the presenting problem." Alina states, "My natural thought process is very much in line with the solution-focused approach, so it resonated with me the best. In addition, I can also say that thinking systemically simply makes sense to me and also resonates with the way I naturally see the world and approach complications in my professional and personal life. I would say that my job chose me; through personal breakthroughs and life lessons I would say that I have been on the path to being a therapist my whole life and feel so unbelievably fortunate to be in the position I have found myself in."

About diversity

Idit states, "Growing up in a different country with a different culture and religion (I grew up in Israel as Jewish), was the perfect background for another core value that was a big part of my training as a marriage and family therapist—that would be diversity. Being a part of the diverse population in South Florida, I understand the importance of being aware of cultural, spiritual, and lingual differences as a therapist. This notion has been guiding me in my work with diverse populations, and as a state association board member and the diversity committee chair this past year . . . Since graduating, it has been my mission to promote diversity as part of my profession."

Alina states, "Born in the USSR myself, my diverse cultural background has really helped me develop even more sensitivity towards other cultures. The personal challenges I experienced along with my family have shaped me into the person I am today. Though I was a child when my family immigrated to the US, my parents have shared endless stories of the obstacles they experienced transitioning to this country and the culture. I am able to use my knowledge, education, and personal experience to help

"Context also plays a vital role in my therapeutic approach. Understanding that everything makes sense in context allows me to be even more curious and sensitive, as opposed to being critical or taking an expert stance. The training I received provided a foundation for my career and with time I have learned even more through educational seminars, workshops, books, and work experience. I refer to my approach as eclectic—drawing from so many theories and approaches!"

ALONSO'S STORY

Alonso Manns, Established Practice, Large Urban Area

Background

Alonso is a licensed marriage and family therapist, and a state qualified supervisor. He has also completed a certificate in human resource management. He is the owner/manager of a private practice incorporated as an LLC, and at present four other clinicians are contracted to work in his practice. Alonso's practice is United Therapists of South Florida.

What is this job like?

Alonso works with individuals, couples, and families. He comments, "The issues that I help clients address include, but are not limited to: marital conflict or relationship distress; family discord and parenting issues; anxiety, trauma, and depression; communication skills; workplace conflict and distress; pre-marital counseling; and Employee Assistance Program counseling. I also offer clinical supervision for licensure to MHC/MFT interns, and occasionally will have interns work in my office for onsite supervision. Since my practice is incorporated as an LLC, I manage all administrative and financial aspects as well." Over time, he has found himself working with more and more workplace issues, which has become a particular interest of his, hence his decision to pursue the additional certification in human resource management.

How do you get a job like this?

Alonso worked for a private nonprofit agency for seven years, rising to increasingly responsible supervisory positions. He comments, "I had always wanted to be a small business owner. So, after working in nonprofit mental health services for seven years prior, and becoming burned out by dynamics beyond my control, I left my employer and immediately put plans in place to develop my own private practice. Approximately a year later, my practice was finally operating at a profit." Alonso suggests that others thinking of taking the same plunge prepare ahead of time. He suggests a step process:

1   Save money towards opening costs. This will add up over the minimum 2–3 years it takes to become licensed and work on your own.
2   Identify 2–3 other graduates who also want to eventually work in private practice. Starting a practice will be easier with other therapists.
3   Identify clinical areas that interest you and begin to read/train in these areas now! You will need to be able to differentiate yourself from the herd of other therapists who are in private practice now, or will be entering it in the future—the more specific the better. Clients will still seek you out for general issues as well.
4   Do not be afraid to accept insurance reimbursement, no matter what other clinicians say. During economic downturns, people cut non-necessities like therapy. People with insurance are definitely more likely

to engage in therapy, particularly middle- and lower-income people. You should look for insurance panels and EAP providers that may allow you to join their panels shortly after licensure. This may be difficult, but can be overcome if the therapist has accrued specialized experience since graduation.

5   Finally, incorporate as a business. This will be advantageous at tax time, when you have begun private practice work.

What is most rewarding?

Alonso states, "The most rewarding thing about my job is the fact that I know my time and energy spent working with people in this context truly does make a difference, and that the result of people moving to a healthier emotional place will have positive effects in other areas of society. The work that a therapist does in the present can make a difference one or two generations into the future!"

What is most challenging?

While enthusiastic about the rewards, Alonso is equally clear about the challenges. "The biggest challenge that a professional faces in private practice is dealing with an unknown/uncertain job landscape. People's need for and commitment to therapy is always in flux, and beyond the control of the clinician. This makes for a business that can be unpredictable, and requires a clinician to be exceptionally attuned to business cycles, threats, opportunities, and changes. Like driving a manual car, therapists in private practice have to be able to shift gears effectively between marketing and seeking new business, to attending to the current groups of active clients. Furthermore, clinicians have to have the discipline and dedication to invest whatever time is necessary to ensure profitability of their practice, and resist the temptation to 'skip' work without considering budget, missed referrals, and consistency of care for clients."

What about your MFT training is most helpful to you?

Alonso feels he was particularly influenced by both systemic thinking and brief therapy models. "Because I do view situations systemically, and not linearly, I find myself doing very good work with couples, entire families, and people who are having issues at their place of employment. With workplace issues in particular, many people don't realize that they are in a relationship not just with peers, superiors, or subordinates, but also with the organization as a whole. People who simply take a linear perspective of these contexts often only exacerbate whatever problems exist. I am particularly fond of the MRI/Strategic model, and the concept of the negative recursive cycle of interaction resonates with the majority of clients.

The problematic interactions between spouses, coworkers, or within families can literally be 'mapped out' for clients to see, which seems to make an impact."

About diversity

Alonso has a deep personal commitment to diversity issues, stemming from personal experiences. "Since diversity and inclusiveness are very dear, personal issues for me, I actively solicit clients who have situations centering on cultural/multicultural issues. When working with clients, I routinely assess for underlying, active cultural/diversity issues that the client isn't aware of. Sometimes, even family or corporate cultures are more influential than clients realize, particularly for those engaged in a conflictual work or family system."

JULIEN'S STORY

Julien Faure, Established Private Practice, Small Town Setting

Background

Julien is currently working in a private practice in eastern Oklahoma as a counselor/therapist. Julien previously worked as an attorney, but private practice is his first position as a therapist.

What is the job like?

Julien specializes in work with children. Julien successfully combines his work as a private practitioner with working in schools. Most of Julien's clients are children, so during the school year he goes to schools during the day and sees more children at the office after school.

How do you get a job like this?

Julien reports that he augmented his practice when he "answered an ad in the newsletter of the school where I was taking extra classes to be licensed in Arkansas." Julien lives in Arkansas, close to the Oklahoma border. In his graduate internships, he worked with children in schools.

What is most rewarding?

Noting some of the most salient rewards of a private practice, Julien says, "Being able to do what I love. I don't see what I do as a job but as a career. I see myself being a therapist for a long time."

41

What is most challenging?

Julien reports that it can be a challenge to involve client families: "This is especially true when a school refers a client to me. The school sees that there is a problem, but the family does not necessarily see that there is a problem, therefore they are less likely to be involved." Julien also shares a struggle common to many therapists. He mentions, "Not knowing if I am doing the 'right' thing. As therapists we provide a service, so it is difficult to gauge if we are providing the most appropriate service to the client at the time. It is even more difficult with younger clients as they are less likely to be able to provide feedback."

What about your MFT training is most helpful to you?

Julien notes, "The principles of being curious, respectful, nonjudgmental, and meeting the clients where they are have been most helpful in my practice and adjusting to working in an environment that was unfamiliar to me. During sessions I often remind myself of those principles. I also try to be goal or solution oriented, especially when clients provide problem-saturated stories."

About diversity

Julien has experience in a range of settings. "My training has been especially useful to help me adapt where I work, given my background. I currently work in rural Oklahoma. Less than 9,000 people live in the town where my office is located, and when I visit schools, they may be in villages of a few hundred people. I was raised in France in a mid-sized city and had lived in Miami, FL for the past seven years before moving to Arkansas. So knowledge of context has been important!"

TEQUILLA'S STORY

Tequilla Hill, Private Practice

Background

Tequilla has both a master's and a doctoral degree in family therapy. She is a licensed MFT and AAMFT Approved Supervisor, and has her private practice outside Atlanta, GA. Her practice is Hill Psychotherapeutic Services, LLC.

What is this job like?

Tequilla successfully balances multiple professional endeavors. She states, "Currently, I am the owner of Hill Psychotherapeutic Services, LLC, a boutique private practice in Marietta, GA. My practice provides therapy, coaching, supervision, and consultation services. I am also an Adjunct professor at Northcentral University's Online Marriage and Family Therapy program. Lastly I hold a committee member position at the state level for GAMFT (Georgia Association for Marriage and Family Therapy). I love that I can serve in our profession utilizing my skills as a therapist, supervisor, educator, and advocate."

Tequilla further shares her enthusiasm for what she has created. "My days are dynamic and I love it! I am very structured with my times and appointments which are a mix of supervision or client consultations. The other parts of my week include student coaching and teaching through feedback via technology. As part of her successful practice, Tequilla has found ways to market herself. She calls herself "a social butterfly" and participates in monthly networking and supervision groups. Additionally, she connects weekly with "other female entrepreneurs and MFT entrepreneurs." As stated above, she is active in GAMFT and commits to one speaking engagement a month.

How do you get a job like this?

Tequilla started with private nonprofit agency work and became licensed, exploring new options as she went along. "My current job was a manifestation of my career journey as a therapist. Holding positions in leadership exposed me to a deeper understanding about managed care and the business of therapy. My passion for clinical work and training other therapists led me to intertwining all the things I enjoy into my business. I didn't really have a plan on the onset of my education. I was just curious, open, and passionate about helping people.

"I have held a variety of jobs in the field of behavioral health. I have been a youth and family therapist, crisis phone supervisor, group home therapist, Regional Director, and Clinical Director. I was also a professor at St Leo University and Richmond Graduate University."

What is most rewarding?

Tequilla states that what is most rewarding is "To be able to have full control of how I work as a MFT. I am able to be improvisational, creative, systemic, strength based, and problem solving. The flexibility is great—however, it also takes a great deal of discipline and focus." She adds, "I love that I get to wear the diverse hats of an entrepreneur, therapist, supervisor, and professor. And I am a wife in training, along with being a daughter, aunt, and friend."

What is most challenging?

Tequilla notes, "At times being in private practice could be a lonely place, so it's important to seek colleagues to connect with. I had to be very intentional about building my legion of MFT entrepreneurs to connect with for emotional and business support."

What about your MFT training is most helpful to you?

Tequilla says, "It's simply a part of me. I have been able to apply my understanding of human systems in managed care, self-of-the-therapist supervision, understanding multiple perspectives, and patterns with my clientele. The amazing diversity of couple and family systems and the universal patterns is how they operate. I am integrative in my approach to clinical practice, pulling from Bowen family systems, solution-focused, and narrative approaches. However, my underlying theme in all that I do is always client centered, strength based, and systemic."

About diversity

Tequilla notes, "I have a very diverse client base and have the pleasure of serving people from different cultures, religions, and lifestyles. I am extremely proud of that, seeing that I am a thirty-something female MFT of color practicing therapy in the South where many people are not as open minded about seeking treatment. I find that many of my clients are first-time therapy seekers and often have a long list of questions about the process and what to expect. Many times they have already gone to pastoral counseling and are curious about how therapy can help. I openly share with them that although I did not attend seminary, I am readily able to still embrace and connect with their spiritual principles. I find that connecting with people's spirituality is very important in the South, which is a natural fit for me because I find that spirituality is an empathic way to connect with how our clients organize their lives.

"I am a progressive therapist and I try diligently to create the atmosphere of empathic understanding, curiosity, and empowerment in my work as an MFT. I think this comes from the stance my parents took in teaching me as a child to have an appreciation for difference among people. Today, I carry that appreciation and openness into my clinical, supervision, and leadership work."

KATIE'S STORY

Katie Lemieux, Trainer and Supervisor, Private Practice

Background

Katie is a licensed marriage and family therapist and state qualified supervisor for both mental health counseling and marriage and family therapy interns. She holds a specialization certificate in Medical Family Therapy. She is the owner and director of a private practice called Lemieux Solutions Unlimited, LLC. She has rebranded the practice, which will be debuting later this year. The new brand will be called BrainBoxe. She is also co-owner and co-visionary of K2 Visionaries with Dr. Kate Campbell. She states, "We are a personal and professional development company committed to fulfilling dreams through world-class personal and professional development."

What is this job like?

Katie describes the importance of self-care and how that starts her day. "The first thing I do every morning is my self-care regimen which includes a combination of reading, meditating, and fitness. Starting my day this way ensures two things: I get those important things done, and it's the platform for which I create my life and my businesses. After I complete my self-care regimen in the morning I do a variety of things such as marketing, reaching out to contacts, following up with calls, networking, attending events, trainings, learning, or seeing clients." Katie sees clients four days out of the week. She also supervises every other week on Fridays and Saturdays, and says, "I absolutely love it!"

How do you get this job?

Katie states, "I actually no longer have a job, which is a great thing. I would say that was one of the most nerve-wracking and difficult decisions to make, leave something sure, safe, and secure. I would never turn back." She goes on to reflect on her past experience, which led her to where she is now. "I worked in the nonprofit world for 11 years. I held various positions, from a case manager while I was attending grad school, to Residential Group Home Coordinator, Clinical Program Supervisor, coach and trainer. I became self-employed in November 2012, going into private practice full time."

What is most rewarding?

Katie says she loves working with couples, individuals, teens, and families. She especially loves "to watch people become conscious and aware of things they couldn't previously see that have impacted their life, forever altering and changing their world, life, and relationships. It is a beautiful thing and makes my heart smile." She adds, "I also love working with my interns. I enjoy leadership and helping people grow and develop both personally and professionally. I enjoy helping people fulfill on the things that matter to them most. I am an entrepreneur at heart. If you asked me years ago if I would be a business owner, I would have said, 'No,' and now my businesses are my passion. I love having the ability to make things happen, being as creative as I want to be, and trying new things to see what works."

45

What is most challenging?

Katie articulates the commitment involved in having your own business, along with the joys. "With business, I am always growing and expanding to the next level, so there is always work to do. Sometimes, I think the biggest challenge for any business owner is the conversations we have between our own two ears. The other thing is that we work with people and at times that can be a challenge. For me it is important to have a good support system both personally and professionally, colleagues to reach out to and a commitment to continue to grow. I have done a lot of my own self-work and right now I am three months into a year-long commitment to work with a business coach, and I love it!"

What about your MFT training is most helpful to you?

Katie describes how embedded her training is in the following way: "I never think of my skills and who I am as two distinct parts. I am my skills and my skills are me. I am a therapist. I am curious by nature. I love to learn about others, their worldviews, and their perspectives. I find it interesting and fascinating. The tools we learn as therapists are more valuable than ever imagined. When working with my interns I often remind them of the tools they have and that they can use them across ANY context—business, customer service, sales, relationships, etc. I don't think people realize how valuable our education is. It isn't just for the therapy room."

About diversity

Katie shares, "I tend to attract a lot of women looking for empowerment. I find I work best with clients from 13–55 years old. My age is approximately in the middle of the ages of the clients I work with. As I have gotten older I have decided no longer to work with younger children. Overall, I find that I work with diverse populations very well, as I take the 'one down' always being curious, allowing diverse populations to teach me about their specific culture, perspectives of their culture, and their own familial culture. There have been times that I have not been the best fit for someone and have referred out to identify a therapist who is more suited to what they need, whether that be age, culture, etc."

Chapter 6

About School-Based Settings

Anne Rambo

Only one state (Connecticut) requires the hiring of family therapists in its schools (as guidance counselors are required in all states). Other states (Florida in particular) allow family therapists to be hired by the schools as school social workers are hired: at the discretion of the principal. Even in less welcoming states, some family therapists in private practice contract with individual schools, formally or informally, and private schools may hire family therapists. Our national organization, AAMFT, is lobbying for inclusion of family therapists in schools under the "No Child Left Behind Act." Some creative family therapists have entered the school system through peer counseling programs. Still others have become dually qualified, adding guidance counselor certification to their family therapy credentials. And finally, some family therapists are teachers and principals, and develop private therapy practices on the side, after their school working hours. Salaries are commensurate with other education professionals. We interviewed Philip, a family therapist in the school system; Walter, a family therapist who also qualified as a guidance counselor; and Susy, who works at an alternative school for children with special challenges. We also interviewed Farheen, who uses her family therapy degree to enhance her elementary school teaching.

OUR SUCCESS STORIES RECOMMEND . . .

A teaching certificate is always valued in the school system, even if not required for a particular position. Time in the classroom adds credibility to your advice to teachers. Family therapists are relatively new to the multidisciplinary team, and you will need to explain yourself and your credentials. Family therapists can bring a relational perspective and greatly enhance family/school collaboration. Inclusion is on the rise, and opportunities will continue to expand. As one of our interview subjects, guidance counselor Walter, reminds us, "Systems thinking can be applied to any field, industry, interest, or venture. One can build and operate a business on systems theories, consult various firms with increasing efficiency, reach the

47

community, invent the next technological device, improve political administration, or envision and create a way to use systems theories that we have yet to hear or read about. I already had a knack for education as a teacher. MFT and systems theories helped me become a better educator and opened opportunities for me to embark on various positions within the education system and in the community."

PHILIP'S STORY

Philip Ganci, School-Based Family Therapist

Background

Philip is a licensed marriage and family therapist. He is currently working as a family therapist for a public school designated as an alternative, behavior-intervention school. He has previously taught high school, and also has experience working for private nonprofit agencies.

What is this job like?

Philip notes, "I do a variety of tasks, but my main responsibility is to facilitate individual and group counseling sessions on a daily basis at the school. I mainly work with students who have counseling specified on the IEPs (Individual Education Plans), but I also work with students who have a history of trauma or have been having severe behavioral issues in the classroom. I attend IEP meetings, help create appropriate goals for students, develop classroom behavioral intervention strategies, help with RTI, hospitalize when needed, and perform crisis intervention." Philip also meets with parents and works to support teachers and other educational colleagues.

How do you get a job like this?

Philip had experience in the school system, and experience with at-risk youth. He recommends getting a variety of experience and getting to know people in the school system.

What is most rewarding?

Philip states, "The most rewarding part of my job now is the connection you make with these students and being able to help them achieve their goals. It is a very difficult population, so when you truly reach a kid and can work with them and they trust you, it is a very rewarding experience."

 48

What is most challenging?

No therapist reaches everyone all the time. As Philip says, "The biggest challenges I face now are building rapport with kids who have experienced a lot of trauma, abuse, or who have just been told so many times they are a 'problem,' they believe it themselves. These kids do not trust very easily and breaking down those barriers is very difficult, and sometimes is not possible, which as a therapist could make you feel like a failure. Understanding limits is probably one of the greatest challenges of any therapist."

What about your MFT training is most helpful to you?

Philip finds systems thinking very useful. "I use my training all the time; my whole framework for therapy is built on how relationships affect who we are and how we think. My job is not to impose my values: it is to get to know theirs so that I can truly understand how to help them. I am very thankful for my training: it has allowed me to separate my own values from my clients', and to truly understand how to listen and help someone. Especially in my position now, the last thing my clients need is another person, who is not living their life, telling them what they are doing wrong and how they need to change. I truly believe in systems theory, and the more I practice, the more I see its validity."

About diversity

Philip comments, "I look at myself as a straight male, 31 years old, Italian-American, a husband and a father most importantly. The MFT program and our field have made me more aware of my own beliefs and values, and prepared me to work with diverse populations without letting those beliefs affect how I provide therapeutic services."

WALTER'S STORY

Walter Howard, Family Therapist/Guidance Counselor

Background

Walter has a master's degree in marriage and family therapy, from a COAMFTE accredited program, and initially after graduation worked for a private nonprofit agency, rising to the position of crisis coordinator/director. He has a teaching certificate, however, and prior to his master's, had worked as a math teacher. He had an interest in returning to the educational environment. While his home state does allow the hiring of family therapists in the school system, he felt there would be more opportunities for him if he added the additional certification of guidance counseling. This required him to take 15 additional graduate hours, primarily in the areas of career counseling and test administration. Once this was completed, he became dually credentialed, and was hired as a guidance counselor in the public schools.

What is this job like?

As a school counselor, Walter functions as part of the school's leadership team. He provides individual and group counseling, and also presents guidance-oriented activities in the classrooms. He arranges parent, teacher, and student conferences. He is part of the collaborative problem-solving team (CPS), along with the school psychologist, social worker, teachers, administrators, and educational specialists, who determine the best educational placement for each child. Walter also runs parent groups, and works to involve parents in the life of the school.

How do you get a job like this?

Walter applied through the school district, where he was already known as a former teacher and as a family therapist in the community. He was offered a position the same day he applied.

What is most rewarding?

In Walter's experience, "the most rewarding part of my job is encouraging youth in a socially and economically depressed demographic. Furthermore, co-creating an alternate, healthy, and constructive perspective of life, goals, potential, and possibilities to students who are very impressionable. Knowing that my influence, words, value, and passion are influential is truly rewarding."

What is most challenging?

It is a challenge for Walter when students fail to respond—he stresses the importance of determination and perseverance in trying to turn around a student's poor school performance. As a family therapist, Walter also has a unique perspective, and values contact with family therapy peers outside the system. Finally, he notes it can be challenging to meet the needs of students, parents, and school administrators, all at the same time.

What about your MFT training is most helpful to you?

Walter tells us, "I use systems thinking, understanding that inserting myself in my students' system changes the dynamic of the system. I like to think of myself as a resource, evoking first-order change through reframing, conventional and paradoxical interventions, tracking student progress, and follow-up. I also employ cognitive behavioral techniques, co-creating measureable and attainable goals, e.g., having a good day (being on time, proper uniform, book bag, positive/respectful attitude, etc. . . .), and tracking them. Reframing is also a valuable technique to use when teachers are frustrated and consumed by negative talk and thoughts. Students are receptive to reframing when you are helping them put their academic and social goals and priorities into a relative perspective."

About diversity

Walter adds that "respect for diversity is one of the most pertinent core values of MFT that I incorporate every day. There are teachers and leadership personnel from various ethnic backgrounds in addition to religious, sexual orientation, professional training (traditional and contemporary), and students from various ethnic and socioeconomic statuses." It is important to "meet others where they are," especially in meetings when so many professional opinions, directives, and perspectives present themselves. With regard to the student population, "the joining process is important for building rapport and trust."

SUSY'S STORY

Susan Peck Lauderdale, Alternative School Family Therapist

Background

Susy works at an innovative program which treats teenage boys who have entered the legal system for one reason or another, but primarily for substance abuse. She is the primary therapist for these young men. The program is a combination of vocational training and mental health counseling. Susy is an LMFT, but has not needed any educational credentials, with this alternative/at-risk population.

What is this job like?

Susy vividly describes a typical day in her atypical setting: "My office is in an auto mechanic garage and I love it. I get to provide therapy in a closed office, one on one, or have a supportive/informative/therapeutic conversation while making T-shirts, working on a car, making a picnic table, or making fishing lures."

How do you get a job like this?

Susy interned in an alternative school setting, dealing with a similar population. She was hired after graduation. When that job proved limiting, she moved to this new program.

What is most rewarding?

Susy has learned to treasure each positive step. As she notes, "When I entered graduate school, I had a pretty good idea that I wanted to work with children, especially teenagers. However, I did not expect that I would gravitate towards working with this specialized population. It is both extremely challenging and rewarding. The best advice I got when I first started working with these kids was 'baby steps'. I had to quickly redefine my idea of success. Sometimes the success looks like an elimination of arrests or a decrease in Baker Acts or just increasing the student's motivation to come to school every day, or providing a positive adult attachment that will allow them to improve their relationships in the future. When working with a teenage population, being genuine is imperative . . . they can smell it when you are not being real with them. Once in a while, you get the honor of knowing you played a part in helping the client achieve their goals."

What is most challenging?

The school system itself can be punitive, and it is important for a therapist to be able to maintain a neutral position, not over aligning with the school, yet cognizant of the needs of school officials as well. This can be a challenge.

What about your MFT training is most helpful to you?

Susy cites systems thinking, a focus on relationships, and the ability to collaborate as critical skills.

About diversity

Cultural awareness is a critical skill in working with teenagers. Susy adds, "I would also say that you need to be aware of your own biases and make sure that your awareness informs your therapy. Some of these students come from very challenging backgrounds including, but not limited to, extreme abuse and neglect, culture of poverty, dysfunctional family systems, to name just a few; we see it all. A working knowledge of the dominant cultures in your community is also beneficial. When there are instances of 'not knowing,' I am always up front with the client about my knowledge, or lack, of their cultural beliefs. This usually prompts a good conversation on how I can be most helpful to them. Finally, have a thick skin. There will most likely be times when you will be called every name in the book and even have to duck flying objects like computers, books, desks, or chairs. When they are at their least lovable is when you have to love them the most."

FARHEEN'S STORY

Farheen Jayatilleke, Elementary School Teacher

Background

Farheen has a master's degree in family therapy. Her internship was school based, and she became interested in working within the school setting. She collaborated with teachers and saw the importance of their role with children. She decided to make the move into full-time teaching. She was recently awarded Teacher of the Year by her school.

What is this job like?

As an elementary school teacher, Farheen has multiple roles. As she describes it, "I have to be a leader, a team member, a nurturer, and a mediator as well as an educator."

How do you get a job like this?

Right after graduation, Farheen was doing in-home family therapy for a private nonprofit agency, but when an opportunity opened up to substitute teach at one of the schools she worked with, she took it. She then obtained a temporary teaching certificate and is now working on a permanent one. She has found the skills she learned as a marriage and family therapist transferable and helpful.

What is most rewarding?

Farheen comments, "I love my job for several reasons. I believe it is the best job for my personality type. It allows me to be creative, to use my organizational and time management skills, and to take on a leadership role. Furthermore, my job is amazing because I get to work with children and their families. I get to be the person who teaches them new skills and that is very rewarding to me. I help them obtain the tools necessary to succeed."

What is most challenging?

It can be challenging to work within the often overtaxed school system. However, good communication helps, as does a systemic perspective.

What about your MFT training is most helpful to you?

Farheen uses a solution-focused orientation in her classroom, as she did in her therapy. She explains, "Much of what I learned (as a family therapist) has also helped me with my classroom management. For example, solution-focused brief therapy teaches clients to set small reachable goals. I have often applied that technique to my students. Of course, I have to modify it to fit the needs of my classroom. However, the ideals are the same rather than focusing on the symptoms that are labeling the student as a bad child, we focus on the goal (i.e., keeping his hands and feet to himself) and how the student is successful in achieving steps to his goal." Farheen also stresses systemic thinking, and staying open and curious. She adds, "We learn so much from our master's program and it can be useful in various fields and work environments. So why not branch out and use those skills in an environment where you will be happy? Ultimately, it's our passions that make us successful and fulfilled in life."

About diversity

"I am a 26-year-old woman. Although I identify myself as American because I was born and raised here, my parents are from India and Pakistan. Having roots in a different culture affects my work because it helps me understand that family beliefs can impact student perspectives on education. It allows me to meet the children (and families) where they are at. And that helps me understand how to help them move forward in their academic progress."

Chapter 7

About Collaborative Settings with Other Professions (Medicine and Law)

Tommie V. Boyd

With their systemic, relational orientation, marriage and family therapists are ideally situated to collaborate with other professions. Collaboration with medical professionals, especially in the area of family medicine, is often called family systems healthcare. Resources to learn more about these endeavors can be found at www.cfha.net. Collaboration with attorneys around family law matters is referred to as collaborative law. Resources to learn more can be found at www.collaborativepractice.com. Individual medical practices and law firms also contract with marriage and family therapists for unique collaborations. Our success examples here are Brian, who works for a large medical practice, and Randy, whose private family therapy practice works in conjunction with collaborative attorneys.

OUR SUCCESS STORIES RECOMMEND . . .

Brian puts it concisely when he says, "First learn the language of the system where you wish to work. Use your skills to translate what you have learned into the practical business world. I have met some MFT grads who are so excited and they end up trying hard to convince others to see things in their way; they want others to join them inside their box. The key is spending time in someone else's box and understanding their reality." In order to collaborate with other professions, we as marriage and family therapists are the ones who need to learn the language of the other professionals, just as we learn and use the language of our clients.

BRIAN'S STORY

Brian Rosenberg, Corporate Director of Training and Development

Background

Brian is Director of Training and Development for a large medical management company. His organization owns and manages physician practices around the United States, with a current total of 2,000 physicians and 10,000 employees.

What is this job like?

Brian explains: "On a daily basis I work with business executives and high-level physician executives to help them in solving complex teamwork, interpersonal, conflict, and medical group governance challenges. I also design leadership development meetings and activities to help effectively transition associate bedside physicians into leadership roles in their practice and in the larger organization. Succession planning, organization development, coaching, problem solving, and general activities that engage the system and develop the employees are items that show up on my desk on a daily basis."

How do you get a job like this?

Brian's dissertation for his doctorate in family therapy was on systemic organizational consulting, and this was his introduction to this field. He also systematically set about to learn business vocabulary, interviewing the dean of a business school and learning what words (like "therapy") not to use. He began as a consultant to a large hospital district, and has remained in organizational consulting.

What is most rewarding?

Brian identifies that the "most rewarding parts of my job come from helping people manage the complex relationships within their work lives. I get great satisfaction in helping people see their exact situation in other ways and in ways that help them gain flexibility, enthusiasm, and positive energy to complete their work tasks. I would imagine the rewarding factors that I list in my job are very similar to what a working MFT therapist might say—my clients are just different and my interactions are different."

What is most challenging?

Brian must constantly demonstrate how his training and development functions affect the bottom line—this is the corporate, business aspect to his job. In doing so, he develops training and mentors those at the various medical centers to advance their skills and remain successful, contributing medical professionals.

What about your MFT training is most useful to you?

Brian sees a close relationship between his training and what he does now. "Systems thinking, natural systems theory, brief therapy modalities and the use of thoughtful questions are all used in my work to help people make better sense out of their situation. One hundred percent of my work is relational. One person's behavior in surgery directly impacts everyone else. How one nurse interacts with her medical director or nursing leadership will be recognized by the patients and everyone else. I can't think of an instance where the tools, methods, theories are not directly impacting my professional life."

About diversity

Brian reflects on how diversity impacts him and his work: "Diversity is a very important factor that I consider in all of my work. If I am working with a team where some section of the group thinks differently from other sections of the group, this dynamic could lead to conflict and tension. A reframe that I use to guide everyone away from conflict is the concept of organizational diversity. It is of critical importance to the organization to have multiple perspectives and multiple points of view all coalescing towards a resolution. Working with physician executives adds another important factor related to diversity and that is educational and IQ. Some physicians believe that they know all of the answers and know the best outcomes to any and all issues. Some are supremely confident and this could lead to poor listening and weak problem solving. The key is using diversity to open the floor to multiple opinions and multiple perspectives in hopes of creating a collaborative agreed-upon decision."

RANDY'S STORY

Randy Heller, Interdisciplinary Collaborative Family Law Specialist

Background

Randy has a multilevel group of practice areas, licensed as a LMFT and LMHC, and a doctoral degree in MFT. She is also a Certified Supreme Court Family Mediator, Qualified Parenting Coordinator, Trained Collaborative Facilitation, qualified hypnotherapist, as well as holding an adjunct faculty position at a local university. She is founder, owner, and director of a collaborative counseling center, working with divorcing couples and families.

What is this job like?

Randy explains, "My work as a collaborative divorce facilitator includes working with a team of professionals—legal and financial—to assist families moving through a divorce. Divorcing parents look to this team to assist in resolving the legal and financial issues related to their divorce, developing a parenting plan, time-share agreement, and becoming successful post-divorce co-parents.

"In addition, as a clinician, I work with individuals, couples, children, and/or families transitioning through divorce or any of life's challenges. Outside of the 'therapy room,' I am engaged in a multitude of activities that develop my practice and my career. All of these areas provide tremendous networking possibilities. I sit on the board of three professional organizations in the field of collaborative practice. I also serve as a consultant for many professionals beginning to work in these processes.

"I speak nationally and internationally about working with families in divorce as a marriage and family therapist and in other roles, and I teach at the university. I wrote the syllabus and developed the first course in the nation (perhaps the world) for mental health professionals working in the area of divorce, specifically but not limited to collaborative divorce, and am educating the next generation of family therapy masters and doctoral students to assist these families."

How do you get a job like this?

Randy has a background as a school-based family counselor, which first exposed her to the effects of divorce on children. From there, she moved into private practice and the specialized collaborating-with-the-family law field.

What is most rewarding?

Randy reflects, "Watching them grow and emerge more fulfilled and satisfied with life is a wonderful motivating experience not only for the people I work with, but for me."

What is most challenging?

Randy notes, "My greatest challenge is accepting that people's readiness to change comes at different times and at a different pace than I might want for them. I respect that change is quite difficult. There are times when I can see beyond a person's challenges when they cannot. I recognize that I must meet the client where they are and allow them to move at their own rate of speed." This is a common challenge for therapists. Particular to her area of practice, although also familiar to many therapists, is this problematic aspect of divorce: "Parents in the divorce process who are so riddled with anger and pain that they cannot see beyond it and focus on the needs of their children."

What about your MFT training is most helpful to you?

Randy relies on systems thinking in her work. She comments, "From early on in my career, as far back as being a teacher, I recognized that sustainable change cannot occur in a vacuum. I realized that although I worked with an individual, I must consider and include all of the contexts within which they live and interact, in order to effectuate change."

About diversity

Randy draws on her own experiences in her work. She comments, "I understand that my family history, coming from a family with considerable strife and divorce, has much to do with my belief in the human spirit and people's ability to move beyond their circumstances and emerge successful, in spite of everything. I rely very strongly on finding the good, the strengths in every person that I work with, because I truly have confidence that we can find them in everyone. I believe that people are resilient. I also remember not to judge people who come from different backgrounds, cultures, and experiences that I may not understand or be familiar with, because I recognize that all behavior makes sense in context. If I can remain mindful of that, I can see beyond what is in front of me, no matter how disturbing or uncomfortable it may be, and in doing so, help my clients to do that as well."

Chapter 8

About Coaching

Martha Gonzalez Marquez

Coaching is a relatively new area of interest to marriage and family therapists and other mental health professionals, but also to those from business or health backgrounds. Coaching is usually understood as brief sessions between a coach and a client, focused on a set goal. The process is more strictly goal focused than psychotherapy, and the process of becoming a coach involves more training as well. Coaching has much in common, however, with brief, problem- and solution-focused models of family therapy. Coaching is not regulated by any state, although voluntary credentialing bodies exist. Coaches are most often career coaches, college coaches (often called independent educational consultants), marriage and relationship educators, parenting coaches, health and wellness coaches, and executive/business coaches. Some call themselves generic "life coaches," but fewer than 8 percent with the life coach job title make a full-time living at the profession (thebillfold.com/2014/10/life-coaching-for-life-coaches-why-im-quitting/). In the absence of regulation, coaching has become an area where consumers should take great care in choosing a coach. But appropriately credentialed coaches can provide valuable services to their clients. Credentialing organizations that are voluntary and independently evaluate coursework and experience include: the National Association for Career Development (www.ncda.org); the Independent Educational Consultant Association (www.iecaonline.com); the National Council on Family Relations, which credentials family life educators (www.ncfr.org); the American Council on Exercise, which credentials health coaches (www.acefitness.org); and marriage/relationship education sites that offer credentialing as relationship educators (www.smartmarriages.com and www.healthymarriageinfo.org). As the profession is not regulated at present, no license is required, but licensed marriage and family therapists may have more credibility with clients, although they cannot provide both therapy and coaching services at the same time.

Those who are not licensed must be extremely clear they are not providing therapeutic services. We interview a dating/relationship coach (Alex); a dating coach who works with an online dating service (Gaby); a coach specializing in work with car dealerships (Katia); and a career counselor and coach (Trish).

OUR SUCCESS STORIES RECOMMEND . . .

Gain specific coaching credentials to augment your credibility and expertise. Advertise clearly what you do, and how it is different from therapy. Refer out those clients who need more intensive services or who are not a fit with the coaching format. Be creative, and meet the needs of clients in less traditional settings.

ALEX'S STORY

Alex Jones, Dating/Relationship Coach

Background

Alex is a licensed marriage and family therapist. After graduating with her master's, she worked in a research-based private nonprofit program. However, she wanted to try something more entrepreneurial, and she observed a need in the dating/relationship area. She is now a dating/relationship coach and CEO of her own private coaching business, LoveJones, LLC.

What is this job like?

Alex has a varied work schedule. As she describes, "I have marketing days and client days. On the marketing days, I attend different networking events around the city or visit informal social events with the intent on meeting new clients and/or new professional connections. On my client days, I have virtual and phone coaching calls that last between 45–60 minutes in which we follow up on previous tasks, identify any challenges, and develop new goals. A full day is approximately 5–6 calls. Between calls, I am texting and emailing clients new tasks or words of encouragement. I also speak at different group events on a monthly basis, providing tips on attracting 'Prince Charming'."

How do you get a job like this?

Alex states that from her first day of graduate school, she knew she wanted to use her degree in "a creative, non-traditional way." She was willing to take the risk to start her own business.

What is most rewarding?

Alex finds it rewarding when her clients shift their view of the problem, and when they take the first small step towards finding love.

What is most challenging?

Alex identifies, "In my field clients usually begin with a 'There's just no good men/women left' attitude. Shifting this belief can be a bit tough at times but it's a challenge I welcome."

What about your MFT training is most helpful to you?

Alex credits her systems thinking and diversity training as central to relating to clients. She also uses the solution-focused model to focus her clients on present, achievable goals.

About diversity

"I identify as an African-American female, early 30s. This has yet to affect my work. I believe it's because love is universal." Alex focuses on diversity in relationships with her clients.

GABY'S STORY

Gabrielle Azulay, Matchmaker/Coach

Background

Gaby graduated with her master's degree in marriage and family therapy, and found herself frustrated—her first jobs in the field (for private nonprofit agencies) involved domestic violence and substance abuse, and did not satisfy her desire to work with couple dynamics. She had a particular interest in the world of dating. A friend introduced her to an entrepreneur who was running a dating site, and her credentials helped her get that job.

What is this job like?

Gaby is Community Director for Sparkology, an invitation-only dating site for young professionals. She activates memberships, approves applications, and answers customer service questions. She also writes blogs on relationship topics, and gives dating advice to those seeking to improve their profiles.

63

How do you get a job like this?

Gaby has a great story to tell about finding this job. "I have always had a passion for gender dynamics, the dating world, and relationships. I first came into the marriage and family field because I knew I wanted to help others find love and I felt having the credentials would help my credibility and make it easier to find a job in my field. I quickly realized that there was a lot more to the degree. I found myself dealing with substance abuse, domestic violence, and other various topics that strayed far from my original goal. After worrying that I chose the wrong degree, a friend introduced me to an entrepreneur who was interested in having someone take over his dating site. He loved the fact that I had a degree in marriage and family therapy and thought I was the right fit. He believed in me, thanks to my credentials and passion."

What is most rewarding?

Gaby enjoys writing the blogs and researching relationship topics. She loves helping others find love, and feels this is the job she has always wanted. "I love writing for the blog and researching on relationships. I love giving others advice and helping them as best I can to find love. Knowing that I am helping others find love and happiness helps me feel better about myself. I truly found the job I was looking for."

What is most challenging?

The challenges for Gaby came before this job, when she almost gave up on finding her dream job. Now she feels she is making a difference and it is very rewarding for her. She adds, "Don't give up on your dream. The degree is extremely versatile. Keep that in mind! Don't think you are limited to a therapy room."

What about your MFT training is most helpful to you?

Gaby notes, "I think systemically when responding to questions and giving advice or guidance. I put myself in their world and accept their reality. This degree taught me to be open minded and it trained my mind to better understand their goals, needs and desires."

About diversity

Gaby states, "I am a 27-year-old female of a mixed ethnic background. My mother grew up in America, while my dad is from Israel. Honestly, I find that my age affects therapy and interacting with my clients more than my ethnicity or any other factor. I feel people are apprehensive about my age because I am on the younger side. Hopefully this will get better with time. Thankfully I don't encounter this problem as much as I used to because I am able to help others through a computer screen."

KATIA'S STORY

Katia Tikhonravova, Sales Coach, Automotive Industry

Background

Katia is a recent graduate with a master's in marriage and family therapy. While still in her graduate program, she created her coaching business, combining her newfound family therapy knowledge with her former career as a car salesperson. She founded Corporation Clinic, Inc. and together with Shaheed Khan she wrote a book titled *The Calm before the Sale: Calm-Driven Selling Secrets of a Successful Car Salesperson* (Tikhonravova & Khan, 2015). She is employed by car dealerships, providing training and coaching for their sales professionals and managers, especially those on track to be promoted. She has recently also begun offering a car broker service to prospective car buyers, negotiating the car deals for them. Providing a car broker service is a creative way to start a conversation with decision-makers at the car dealerships and begin relationships as a business.

What is this job like?

Katia attends car industry conventions, expos, conferences, and networks with dealerships. She hosts a business YouTube channel, educational events, and webinars. She is an active member of FIADA (Florida Independent Automotive Dealer Association) and NADA (National Automotive Dealer Association). A typical assignment at a dealership might look something like this: "In the dealership, the first step is to meet with the director and discuss what his or her goal is for the car sales professional. Once the goal is clear, then I meet with the car sales professional over the span of two to three months and complete an individual assessment. During my sessions, I assess the goals of my client, the sales person. Typical topics discussed include: What motivates you? What is your miracle for yourself and the company? What do you see as your next step?" Katia uses her systemic therapeutic skills in this setting.

How do you get a job like this?

Katia has combined her previous life experience with systems thinking, family therapy ideas, and coaching training. She recommends building on what you know.

What is most rewarding?

Katia states, "I have had a passion for cars since a young age. I had also been employed in the car industry prior to my MFT degree. Due to this, I decided to combine my passion for cars with my knowledge of solution-focused and Bowen family systems approaches to assist others in achieving personal and professional successes." She enjoys being able to combine her two worlds.

What is most challenging?

Katia is very enthusiastic about having found her niche. As she says, "Follow your passion! If you love what you do, everything else will fall into place. Do not be afraid to put yourself out there, even if you have to try different things to find where you belong, because eventually something will stick. I love and breathe cars, so for me this is exactly the business I want to work in. It is also beneficial to have family and friends who support your goals." With that support, she feels she can overcome any challenges.

What about your MFT training is most helpful to you?

Katia credits systems thinking, respect for diversity, and both solution-focused and Bowenian ideas.

About diversity

Katia explains, "I grew up in the Siberian town of Tomsk in Russia. My family encouraged my sister and me to learn about the mechanics of a car and drive a stick shift as soon as we could see behind the steering wheel. I did not know it was against gender stereotypes for women to sell cars or be interested in cars until I started working at the car dealership.

"I work with a predominately male population. Therefore, I want to discuss my client's possible biases and discomfort about working with a Caucasian female coach in her late 20s as soon as possible. This way 'elephants' can leave the room and we can start working. Most of the time, sales professionals and managers cooperate in coaching sessions despite our differences.

"I often use my nationality as a motive to talk about client's nationality, race, and other aspects of diversity. I ask clients how their diversity affects their relationships at work, life, and with car buyers. Dealerships provide diversity training to their employees. However, as a bisexual in a heterosexual relationship and an LGBTQ community activist, I enjoy hosting short diversity trainings, such as 'Straight advice from gay clients' or 'What does sex have to do with car selling?' to encourage sales professionals to discuss questions they may have about gender, sexual orientation, and other diversity topics, to help them reach their goals."

TRISH'S STORY

Patricia (Trish) Turner, Career Counselor and Coach

Background

Trish Turner has a master's degree in marriage and family therapy. She now has her own business in career counseling and coaching.

What is this job like?

Trish coaches clients who have various goals in mind. "People from all experiences find coaches to support them in their self-discovery, and in their quest to achieve more in their personal or professional lives. So I am constantly seeking ways to help clients reach their full potential by searching for the core hunger, drive, and desire in each of them. I desire to help you find out who you really are, while you discover what you can become: services now extend to students needing to improve or struggling with college decisions, teachers and supervisors hoping to inspire, and others trying to make their mark in the world. On a day-to-day basis, I deal with students trying to determine their next move." She adds, "My idea of coaching is helping the average person embrace and attain greater success, happiness, and comfort in their lives by creating a fitting, intentional path to their own goals." In addition, Trish added to her coaching expertise when she realized "a demand for ethics coaching for human services workers. The ethics courses I taught at the University of Phoenix for health and human services students afforded me an advantage in seeing the value of coaching clients through the processes of ethical standards in their field."

Trish shares, "I subscribe to a solution-focused coaching approach, with an occasional narrative insert. Since clients lean towards a fast fix to their issues, the goal setting, solution-oriented methods work well for my clients. They set the time frame based on their goals, but I ask for a minimum of three sessions."

How do you get a job like this?

Trish spent the years prior to enrolling in her master's degree as an entrepreneur, publishing books and magazines. Realizing the isolation involved in that work and also her affinity for interacting with people and helping families, Trish then embarked on her master's degree. She believes her journey through her varied employment settings and her education in MFT heightened her appreciation for coaching and gave her the necessary background to succeed. Trish's past experiences have included working for agencies as a therapist and as a social worker for the Florida Sheriff's Youth Ranches, assessing "the suitability of mildly delinquent youth and their families to determine if the child would be a good fit for a one-year residential program." She then spent the "next nine years in different state (non-sworn) investigator positions." She joined "different investigative departments; including real estate, agriculture, and consumer services, office of Inspector General for Children and Families, the Lottery, and ultimately the Department of Homeland Security."

Trish evaluated her own employment settings and the aspects she enjoyed within each. What she learned from her own experiences, as well as from her MFT education, led her to create the Career Counseling and Coaching practice. "Career counseling and coaching made sense to me." She adds that although there are no coaching requirements in her state, she did pursue solution-focused training to further her expertise.

What is most rewarding?

Trish notes, "Getting to do what I consider relevant, and what I really enjoy, makes my worklife a dream. The aspect that I find most inspiring is the integrity group sessions I recently incorporated into my coaching practice. I am amazed at the conceptions human service workers and others hold on to about what is acceptable. To see the change in perspectives and the personal growth of professionals, gives me a greater joy than I could have imagined. In addition, seeing clients make steps towards the success they thought was impossible—that's what I live for."

What is most challenging?

Trish shares what many business owners in all fields realize. "I find the biggest challenge to success is having to be constantly available to clients, while seeking new marketing venues, attending functions decidedly aimed at 'getting business' and of course balancing it all. I constantly revise things like flyers, Instagram pages, blogs, and business cards to make sure I stay on top of trends and changes in my financial goals."

What about your MFT training is most helpful to you?

Trish says, "I believe coaching is a growing, evolving, relatable field and an option for therapists . . . My education and therapy degree was instrumental in my confidence in the investigative field and my enthusiasm for working with coaching clients." Trish also resonates to the solution-focused approach.

About diversity

This is an important value for Trish. She notes, "I live in South Florida, so managing a coaching practice that reaches this multicultural population is essential.

 68

What is always in the back of my mind is that each culture is different and members may respond to my coaching messages differently. For example, while engaged in college coaching, I am respectful of the fact that many African-American youths resent being queried about sports and athletic scholarships and are interested in many scholastic areas, including science. One of my first successful clients was a community college student of Haitian descent who was floundering. After letting her guard down and allowing me to remind her of her skills, she soon graduated. I enjoy our multiethnic local culture, but I find it a necessity to be fluent in 'adapting' to be successful in business. So, I tailor my services based on what I have learned (and continue to learn) about individual ethnic groups, equality, fairness, and inclusion."

REFERENCE

Tikhonravova, K., & Khan, S. (2015). *The calm before the sale: Calm-driven selling secrets of a successful car salesperson*. New York: CreateSpace.

Chapter 9

About Military Settings

Anne Rambo

Before 2006, marriage and family therapists were not eligible to be hired by the Veterans Administration—social workers, psychologists, and psychiatrists were the only professions providing mental health services to veterans. In 2006, new legislation mandated the increased hiring of marriage and family therapists, and the American Association for Marriage and Family Therapy (AAMFT) is now partnering with the VA to increase hiring of marriage and family therapists nationwide. Preference is given to those who graduate from COAMFTE accredited programs.

Vet Centers themselves are a relatively new addition to the services offered by the Veterans Administration. They are community-based clinics offering counseling and readjustment services to veterans having difficulty reintegrating in civilian life. In 2003, services were expanded to serve veterans of Iraq and of the global war on terrorism. Family members are now also eligible for treatment. Similar positions are also available in Veterans Administration hospitals, and directly for the Department of Defense, with the Navy, Army, or Air Force. Licensed marriage and family therapists are also hired by mental health agencies that contract with the military, such as Zeiders (www.zeiders.com).

While family therapists are still a new presence in many of these settings, they are encouraged by federal officials to apply, and this is a rapidly growing area of employment. Family therapists must be licensed to be eligible for employment in these positions. The salary range is generally $59,000 to $76,000 annually to start.

OUR SUCCESS STORIES RECOMMEND . . .

Military experience, either directly as a veteran, or indirectly through family ties, is important and valued. The paperwork required to successfully apply to either the VA or the Department of Defense can be cumbersome, and it is recommended to allow three to six months for the application process. Applying widely is also recommended. Once you are hired, hang on to your confidence about being a family therapist and your unique perspective.

We interview two marriage and family therapists who work at Vet Centers, one who is himself a veteran (Anthony) and one with only a family connection to the military (Laura); a marriage and family therapist working for the Department of the Navy (Elissa); one working overseas with the active military (Ronella); and finally a marriage and family therapist who is director of family therapy at a VA hospital (Michele).

ANTHONY'S STORY

Anthony Manfre, Marriage and Family Therapist, Veterans Center

Background

Anthony Manfre was an Army paratrooper with the 82nd Airborne from 1998–2001. He always wanted to join the Army and had dropped out of school after the 9th grade. He envisioned being a paratrooper for ever; however, there came a terrible midair parachute collision that left him legally blind, and resulted in his honorable discharge from the service. He experienced a period of aimlessness, and with his parents' encouragement enrolled in community college to begin earning an undergraduate degree in psychology.

Once he graduated, still feeling unsure about what to do with his life, he became one of only three legally blind individuals to hike the entire Appalachian Trail. During his long hike he befriended a Marine veteran who was also trying to walk his way through his re-entry depression. Anthony became interested in wilderness therapy, and enrolled at Appalachian State University, a COAMFTE accredited master's program in family therapy with a specialization in wilderness therapy. Subsequently, he completed this master's degree and earned a doctorate in family therapy as well. Anthony is now an LMFT and works with veterans at a Vet Center. He was also recently elected as the VA's Southeast Region disability representative; in that capacity he advocates for disabled veterans.

What is this job like?

Anthony sees veterans and their families about four to six hours every day. The rest of his workday, he participates in administrative meetings, and supervision. In addition, at least eight hours a month he provides outreach to the community, visiting colleges and community events to provide education on the Vet Centers and what services are available to veterans.

How do you get a job like this?

Anthony applied for open marriage and family therapy positions on the government's primary employment board (www.usajobs.gov). While there are many positions open, he cautions that he applied to over ten jobs before getting selected. He feels it took him some time to figure out exactly the interview style (performance based, with specifics about previous accomplishments) and resume style that was preferred. He encourages those interested in these positions to apply widely and be patient. The process is time consuming, as he notes: "Once I applied to the job, HR selected my resume and others as the top qualified and sent all of our resumes to the selecting official at the location of the job. The selecting official chooses a handful that she would interview and mine was one of them. The selecting official and some other workers interviewed me and others on the phone. The questions were performance based and the interviewers rated our answers from 0–5. The highest score of all the interviews is sent back to HR where they begin the hiring process. Thus, it could take a month or two for this process and before you are sitting in your new office." While Anthony had previous post master's experience working in community mental health, he feels it was his past military experience that led most directly to his being hired. It was clear he understood firsthand the difficulties veterans can face with readjustment.

What is most rewarding?

For Anthony, it is most rewarding to feel he is still a part of the military family— still connected to those who served.

What is most challenging?

Being new in the system as a family therapist is challenging at times, as Anthony must explain his profession to others.

What about your MFT training is most helpful to you?

Anthony identifies systems thinking and a commitment to diversity as most important.

About diversity

Anthony considers the military its own distinct culture. He had firsthand experience with this reality while working on his dissertation. As he notes, "In listening to the voices of my research subjects (veterans) and beginning to analyze the data, I found that my own experiences as a veteran at times complicated my ability to see larger patterns. While I was definitely hearing the themes of camaraderie among fellow military, coupled with difficulties sharing with 'outside' family members and distrust of authority, it was difficult for me to identify those themes as valid or important. I kept saying to myself (and to my Chair), 'But everyone knows that.' I realized my closeness to the experience of my respondents was causing me to identify with them so completely as to take for granted what they were saying. Mixed in with this closeness may have been a remnant of the unspoken military tradition that the bonds of comrades, so important to those of us in the service, will not be understood by and should not be much spoken of to 'outsiders,' including, in this case, my dissertation Chair and committee. This was something I was able to work through by using discussions with my Chair especially, and by validity checking with respondents, who again emphasized those themes I had at first overlooked as 'too obvious.' While I was able to overcome this difficulty, it may speak to the challenges facing marriage and family therapists without military experience seeking to work with veterans. Those who understand the experience may find it difficult to speak with those who do not share the experience." Anthony hopes to bridge this gap through both practice and research.

LAURA'S STORY

Laura Gales, Marriage and Family Therapist, Veterans Center

Background

Laura became interested in work with veterans after seeing the care her grandfather received from the VA in Miami during his battle with Alzheimer's. She states, "He and my grandmother instilled in me a great respect for those who served our country, as well as those who chose to serve them in their continued battle with the impact of their service." Laura obtained her master's in 2008, and went on to get a doctoral degree in family therapy as well. She is also a certified hypnotherapist.

What is this job like?

Laura provides readjustment counseling services for combat veterans from all wartime eras, and for their families. Due to the needs at her Vet Center, and perhaps also to her training and skill set, her case load is primarily made up of couples (including both veteran and partner in session) and the significant others of veterans who need additional support. She also runs family and relationship-building workshops, which focus on educating and providing support to significant others of veterans coping with PTSD. In addition, she provides couples counseling to veterans who have been victims of Military Sexual Trauma (MST) as they cope with the potential impact of their trauma on their relationship and intimacy. Lastly, she provides bereavement counseling services to the family members of veterans who are killed during their combat service. In addition, she does case management when veterans or their families are having difficulty navigating the VA healthcare and/or benefits system.

How do you get a job like this?

Like Anthony, Laura persevered in applying to open positions. She began applying for jobs with the Department of Veterans' Affairs approximately one year after she got licensed, which was when Congress had just authorized opening positions within the VA specific for licensed marriage and family therapists from COAMFTE-accredited programs. She applied for between 25 and 30 jobs all over the country at both Vet Centers and VA Medical Centers before getting her interview at her present place of employment. She credits her past experience working with a hospice as providing her the experience with veterans that the position required. As she notes, "While working for the hospice I had the honor of working with many World War II and Korean War veterans at end-of-life. This gave me my first exposure to hearing the lifelong impact that their combat service, as well as how the subsequent silence about the trauma they endured, affected them at end-of-life." She recommends marriage and family therapists who are not themselves veterans seek out opportunities to work with this population in other settings, to prepare for VA and Vet Center jobs.

What is most rewarding?

Laura feels a strong sense of purpose in serving veterans and their families. Her commitment to this population makes this a rewarding experience for her.

What is most challenging?

Laura mentions the stigma associated with counseling within the military—something she must overcome with her clients. Additionally, she notes, "Many of the veterans I work with have seen the absolute worst humanity has to offer and some have suffered with that in silence for over 40 years. The stories of trauma and pain can sometimes feel a bit haunting and overwhelming. Luckily, I have been able to find a good group of clinicians both within the VA and my fellow graduates who help me to process the impact of the trauma these men and women share, to ensure that I am able to continue to serve them while managing the possibility of burnout."

What about your MFT training is most helpful to you?

Like Anthony, Laura mentions systems thinking and an appreciation for diversity. The ability to take multiple perspectives is especially important in the work she does with couples; as she describes, "In a basic sense maintaining a focus on multiple perspectives and the basic assumptions of building rapport with multiple family members simultaneously is of crucial importance. When meeting with a couple I am met often with two sets of barriers. With the veteran it is the overall barrier of coming to counseling in the first place, the fear of labeling, and the 'stuckness' that often follows combat service. With the veteran's significant other I am typically facing the assumption that because I work at the Vet Center I will automatically be on the veteran's side. Balancing each of their perspectives and 'truths' as I first establish rapport with a couple allows me to establish a therapeutic relationship built on shared meaning and understanding, as well as helping me to establish goals both individuals can get on board with." This focus on relationship and context helps her be a unique voice within this system.

About diversity

Laura notes, "My social location is that I am a married Caucasian female in my early 30s and recently had my first child. I find that at times my age and gender can be both an asset and a barrier with this population, particularly with veterans who served in the Vietnam War, Korean War, and World War II. Some of these veterans at times have expressed discomfort in working with a civilian who was not even alive when they served in the military. I typically attempt to honor their preference and will offer them an older therapist who served in the military; however, I usually ask them to give me a few sessions to 'win them over.' Those who agree often continue to work with me. I also try to use my lack of veteran status and age to take a position of curiosity about their experience during combat and returning from war. Since I have never been to war and have limited historical knowledge about the wars these men and women served in, I use this to ask questions and allow the veterans to share their individual lived experience with me without attaching my own assumptions. I find that both my age and gender help me take this position in a manner which is nonthreatening and nonjudgmental."

ELISSA'S STORY

Elissa Crist, Clinical Specialist, United States Marine Corps, California

Background

Elissa is a Clinical Specialist for the Marine Corps Recruit Depot. She is a licensed marriage and family therapist and a certified practitioner for rapid resolution therapy.

What is this job like?

Elissa describes, "I provide individual, child/adolescent, family and couples counseling for Marines and their families. Due to this being a Recruit and Training

Depot, I am mostly dealing with drill instructors and their families. I also provide counseling for recruits during boot camp to assist with clearing prior to service abuse, anxiety, depression, and family problems so they can be successful in boot camp and graduate as Marines. I started two groups for recruits that I also conduct on a weekly basis. One group is for recruits who have gotten injured during cycle and are sent to Medical Rehabilitation Platoon (MRP) to heal and return back to cycle. While they are there, I provide groups teaching coping skills and strengthening them emotionally and mentally. I also provide a group at Recruit Separation Platoon (RSP) for recruits who did not make it through boot camp and are being sent home. They generally have a lot of guilt and shame for not graduating and anxiety about their next step. I want to make sure they go home confident and proud of their experiences at boot camp and excited about their next journey."

How do you get a job like this?

Elissa had been in private practice six years when she had a life-changing experience. As she tells the story, "A friend from college came to live with me after finishing her contract with the Army and had PTSD from her deployment to Iraq. Watching her struggle to adjust and hearing about the lack of effective therapeutic services being offered to our military really impacted me. It was then I decided I wanted work with the military." Elissa first got a job with Zeiders as a Child Counselor for Fleet and Family Services; they are a contracted provider with the Department of the Navy. When her current position came open, she applied for it through www.usajobs.gov. She advises beginning therapists to get licensed, and to find what they are most passionate about—becoming specialists, not generalists.

What is most rewarding?

Elissa especially enjoys working with recruits. For many, this is their first time away from home, and there can be severe coping difficulties. Elissa comments, "They are so hungry to move forward and be successful. They are motivated to do the work, soak up the information and are so grateful. I utilize rapid resolution therapy regularly and am seeing amazing, painless, and quick results in clearing trauma. They come visit me after graduation with their parents and thank me as well as send emails with updates. It is extremely rewarding!"

What is most challenging?

Elissa notes the Marine Corps environment is not one in which therapy is automatically accepted. "My biggest challenge is working with a system that is based on the old philosophy of 'sucking it up' and 'being a man.' Marines historically do not seek counseling because they are viewed as 'weak.' I do a lot of outreach, groups, and working hands on with Commands so they get to know me as a person first and feel comfortable. This has resulted in them coming in for counseling and then referring other Marines due to their positive experience. I have slowly begun implementing my groups for recruits, which has never before happened on this base. This greatly helps Commands and so they are in turn supportive and now contact me directly with referrals or to start new groups when they move to a different platoon. This is usually a three-year tour, so Commands are constantly changing and Marines are moving in and out, so breaking down these barriers begins again."

What about your MFT training is most helpful to you?

Elissa identifies systems thinking and respect for diversity, including culture and sexual orientation, as core values from her training that she utilizes daily.

About diversity

Elissa adds, "I am a 36-year-old heterosexual female. Respecting diversity and living in South Florida as I went to school provided me great experience and education about other cultures. This has been extremely useful in the military, which is incredibly diverse. My clients greatly appreciate my knowledge of their culture and sexual orientation. This enables me to teach my colleagues as well."

RONELLA'S STORY

Ronella, * *Clinical Specialist/Clinical Counselor, Marine Corps, Okinawa*

Background

Ronella is a Clinical Specialist/Clinical Counselor for the Marine Corps Community Services (MCCS) under the Department of Defense. She works in the Behavioral Health Branch of the Family Advocacy Department (BHFAP). Ronella is a licensed marriage and family therapist. She is based in Japan.

What is this job like?

Ronella explains, "My daily duties are interesting as I am part clinician, part case manager, and part forensic interviewer. Primarily, I address the needs of the Marine Corp and the Navy communities. The clients I treat are active duty military

* Last name has been withheld by request.

personnel in the Marine Corp and Navy, as well as their dependents. Additionally, we are responsible for treating civilians attached to those military branches. The clients all share common themes: 1) all have an allegation of Abuse or Neglect of a Child or Spouse; 2) they are all mandated for treatment; and 3) they are all attached to or affiliated with the Marine Corp or Navy. I am responsible for conducting assessments, providing treatment, reporting treatment compliance and attendance to Command executive officers or the United States Naval Hospital during treatment, sending referrals to affiliate programs, and providing briefs on our program when needed."

How do you get a job like this?

Before taking her present position, Ronella was already working in Korea as a military family life consultant, serving families and service members in the Army, Navy, Air Force, and Marines. She got her prior job, and her present position, from applying through www.usajobs.gov. Before moving to Korea, and embarking on this work with military families, Ronella worked as an in-home family therapist for a private nonprofit agency. The agency served at-risk youth and also adults with dual diagnosis. Through that work, she became familiar with veterans and issues that they face. She also worked with veterans in her private practice. So she decided to look for a job with military families, and was willing to move overseas. She advises others to be "be open" to possibility.

What is most rewarding?

Ronella states unequivocally, "What is most rewarding to me about my current positon is that I am able to serve a population that protects and serves United States citizens. Our military services men, women, and children do not often get the full extent of what they need in order to function optimally. This position enables me to provide them with a safe place to express themselves, move toward healing the past, and shape a more deliberate and desirable future. I truly value and respect the opportunity to work with individuals who have sacrificed time with their family through deployments; missed extended family connections due to relocations; forfeited a form of stability due to change in duty stations; and risked their lives to protect the United States. This experience provides a richer context for the ability to see the spectrum of challenges that exists within the military population."

What is most challenging?

At times, it is challenging to balance the needs of the individual client with the needs of the military structure. Families must move when needed, due to a change of duty station, even if services must be interrupted.

What about your MFT training is most helpful to you?

Ronella credits systems thinking, and also specific models, including recent marital research. "We currently are studying John and Julie Gottman and use their materials as part of our treatment protocol. The concept of systems thinking reigns supreme over all tools, in my opinion. Since the time I have been here in Okinawa, Japan, I have served families from Philippines, Taiwan, Singapore, Mainland Japan, Okinawa Islands, Nigeria, Ivory Coast, Haiti, Jamaica, Puerto Rico, and across the United States. I have also worked with families that are Buddhists, Christians, Latter Day Saints, Catholics, Muslims, Shinto, Agnostic, and more. I have been fortunate to serve people with diverse backgrounds throughout the course of my work as an LMFT. I apply the idea of curiosity, which is found in the family systems perspective to be very useful in working with people from all over the globe with multilayered stories and perspectives. By utilizing the Gottmans' work, Bowenian family systems, and narrative therapy, I have embraced and celebrated differences as baselines for levels of growth. It has helped me personally and professionally to become more open to the world around me and more appreciative of the things that separate and forge unity as a human race."

About diversity

This is a topic to which Ronella has given much thought, and her comments follow. "I am a heterosexual female of African descent. I do not like to call myself African-American. I prefer the term Black American if I am going to be labeled with any ethnicity. I am human first, last, in between, inside, and out. Really, to call ourselves anything else is less meaningful to me, but I think people enjoy the benefits of 'othering' themselves and other people. I am a mother of four beautiful daughters and I am married to my best friend. I am a practicing Nichiren Buddhist and have been actively chanting Nam-myoho-renge-kyo for over a decade. My clinical work is informed by this philosophy as I allow myself to fully engage in the curiosity that makes the collective human experience unique yet simultaneously universal. That beautiful art/skill, which is the concept of both/and, enriches my life every day. The more I challenge my self-perceptions internally and externally, the more appreciation I have for the journey of others. Mothering allows me to connect with knowing what it means to usher life into the world and appreciating that in clients. Being of African descent has allowed me to connect to culture that is associated with a diaspora of individuals and groups well versed in experiencing trials and tribulations. And finally, being a practicing Nichiren Buddhist gives me the gift of knowing that happiness is and always will be a choice. Through these individual and collective lenses, I can truly be a part of a healing process when I work with clients, because I truly believe anything and everything is possible."

MICHELE'S STORY

Michele,* Therapist, VA Hospital

Background

Michele is a licensed MFT, with a master's and a doctoral degree in the field. Michele is the first marriage and family therapist at a Veterans Affairs Medical Center since 2013, and was the first at Bay Pines VAMC, hired in 2012.

What is this job like?

Michele see clients (couples/families), runs a group twice a month, attends weekly interdisciplinary team meetings, and assists the central office of the VA in DC to educate, advocate, and grow the MFT discipline.

How do you get a job like this?

Michele started out with extensive clinical experience working in agencies for children. She previously worked in military settings as a contractor worldwide, and cites this experience as giving her a unique perspective. When she was ready to quit traveling, she saw this VA hospital position online at wwwusajobs.gov, the main hiring location for military jobs. She has advice for beginning therapists seeking such positions: "Be diligent; get as much experience in different areas as you can in order to make the best decision for you on what direction to take. If you truly want to work for the VA, continue to search USAJOBS (as hiring of MFTs expands there will be future opportunities for internships, pre-licensure positions and eventually supervisory positions), learn about military culture, volunteer at a Veterans' Organization, take free trainings offered on the Internet to learn about active duty and veterans, and search other programs in the community that can utilize your services. Once licensed you can do things like donate an hour, do contractor work, get on insurance panels that service veterans like TRICARE, work at a call center, search jobs with DOD to work with active duty, here and abroad . . . I could go on and on."

What is most rewarding?

Michele describes, "What I started saying when folks asked why I left my own family to travel to live and work on military installations was 'that it was bigger than me' . . . it's hard to explain. The best I can say is that it was not only giving

---

* Last name has been withheld by request.

back or helping my clients (active duty at the time): it was giving back and serving my country as well. I feel the same serving our veterans now." This focus on "bigger than me" is one many military family therapists seem to share.

What is most challenging?

As other have also noted and Michele agrees, "Negotiating the VA/government system. It can be quite daunting even with all the training and assistance they give you. Also, being a trailblazer—they (the VA system) approved MFTs to be hired in 2010 and began hiring in 2012. I am fortunate, yet it is daunting being a 'missionary, trailblazer, taking the road less traveled,' really not sure what to call it . . . Of course I know there are going to be challenges; however, the future is bright, and as I've been told . . . our actions now will positively affect MFTs in the VA long past our time there!"

What about your MFT training is most helpful to you?

"I believe my ace in the hole is our systemic training, hands down . . . it is the reason I changed course after my BS from psychology to MFT and it serves my clients well."

About diversity

Michele shares, "Our veterans come from all walks of life and are very, very diverse. However, when on active duty, they came together as one to defend our country, to protect all we so freely and at times take for granted, those things we are afforded due to their protection. I'd also add that the military has a culture of its own, so if you are already diverse in your thinking, then exploring and being open to learn about their traditions, beliefs, and values positively affects and grows your therapeutic relationship. I currently teach a military family course, and most did not quite understand why I pushed the military culture so much, but this is why—if you know and respect diversity, you will be helpful to all your clients and your sessions will probably go a heck of a lot better. In summation, people know when you're in the trenches with them and when you are not!"

Chapter 10

About Managed Care Settings

Tommie V. Boyd

Managed care and insurance companies hire marriage and family therapists to perform utilization review and assure quality. Our systemic perspective makes us quite valuable in these positions. This is work with the larger system, influencing the entire system of care. A full license is generally required. Application may be made through insurance company websites —www.centene.com, www.cenpatico.com, www.magellanhealth.com, and www.aetna.jobs are examples. Residential treatment centers and hospitals may also have utilization review departments. The salary range is in the higher moderate range, above entry level—typically $50,000 to $70,000 annually. The positions inevitably involve paperwork and the review of others' paperwork. Yet a marriage and family therapist in this position will affect many more clients indirectly than any therapist could by seeing clients directly. This is an opportunity to influence the entire system of care. We interview a utilization review case manager (Anne-Marie), a customer care supervisor (Shazia), and a training manager (Fariha).

OUR SUCCESS STORIES RECOMMEND . . .

Think of yourself as making change in the larger system; your "client" now is the larger system. If you do not have contact with patients, keep your hand in with practice, perhaps a small private practice on the side. Get curious about the world of managed care and health insurance—opportunities to rise beyond utilization review into training and policy exist.

ANNE-MARIE'S STORY

Anne-Marie Rodewald, Intensive Behavioral Health Case Manager/Utilization Review

Background

Anne-Marie is currently Intensive Case Manager (Behavioral Health) for a managed care corporation. Prior to this job, she worked as a family therapist for private nonprofit agencies, gaining experience and becoming licensed.

What is this job like?

Anne-Marie manages the treatment process for those patients who are frequently admitted to hospitals or substance abuse treatment centers. She meets with the patients themselves, and also with reimbursed providers, to determine the best fit and the most appropriate treatment. She is the one who puts together the umbrella of services for each of these high-need clients.

How do you get a job like this?

Anne-Marie watched for openings with major managed care organizations, and networked with colleagues. She was able to point to her experience in the field as providing her a base for treatment decision making. Anne-Marie had experience in psychiatric hospital settings as an intern, and with at-risk youth as an agency therapist. In both those settings, she focused on diagnosis and substance abuse as well as complex systemic understandings. She learned the language of the dominant mental health field as well as systemic/relational understandings, so she could help medical professionals communicate with clients. She also has a private practice specializing in bariatric patients, and works with physicians in this context as well.

What is most rewarding?

Anne-Marie notes a high level of professionalism among her colleagues—"no slackers." She also appreciates the challenge and the high level of responsibility. She feels she is helping the system work as it is meant to work.

What is most challenging?

The job can involve a high volume of referrals, strict deadlines, and rapid changes in available services. The clients are high need and high risk. The pace is fast, and one must stay on top of deadlines and paperwork. It helps to have congenial, committed coworkers. She adds, "A for-profit, managed care/corporate environment can be very competitive, yet also quite rewarding on a personal and professional level."

What about your MFT training is most helpful to you?

The relationship skills and systemic thinking are most valuable to Anne-Marie. She uses her relational and systemic thinking to understand the larger system, and to advocate for the needs of her individual clients. She also utilizes solution-focused, narrative, and intergenerational models of therapy in her work. "Everything that works with the individual client family system also works with the larger system," she notes. Her MFT training helps her work with the entire healthcare delivery apparatus as just another example of a system.

About diversity

Anne-Marie is from Sweden originally, but grew up on an island off the coast of Italy. English is her third language. Having lived in several countries gives her a unique perspective on the United States healthcare system. As she notes, "I can see the larger system. I can see what works, but I can also see the flaws, what could be improved. I know how it is done other places." This broader perspective helps her relate to clients. "I can empathize with their frustrations—I am not that person who has never encountered any snags in life, who can't relate." She considers sensitivity to diversity just as important as academic training in her work.

SHAZIA'S STORY

Shazia Akhturallah, Supervisor Customer Care, Managed Care Agency

Background

Shazia is a licensed marriage and family therapist, with both a master's and a doctoral degree. She has also obtained credentials as a LMHC, Certified Addiction Professional (CAP), and a Fellow Thanatologist (FT). She is currently a Supervisor of Customer Care for a large managed care company.

What is this job like?

Shazia trains and supervises customer care staff of a health plan, for a managed care company. As she explains, "Customer care staff are considered administrative (non-clinical) and are employed by the company to answer phone calls from members and providers about the health plan, such as benefits, authorization, claims inquiries, etc. After they receive the call, they conduct certain tasks such as checking eligibility and benefit, completing health assessments, scheduling appointments for members, looking up billing and claims information, and so on. Their job is to make sure that callers' (including members and providers) needs are met so that they (callers) do not have to call back for the same reason. I supervise them by reviewing and overseeing their work, such as listening to their calls and reading their documentation, conducting individual and team supervision meetings, and providing them feedback, in addition to doing problem solving for complex calls on a daily basis."

How do you get a job like this?

Shazia started out doing home-based work for an agency, and rose to the position of Regional Director for this agency. After licensure and a doctorate, she was hired in utilization review, by the same managed care company for which she now works. Subsequently, the company obtained a contract for integrated behavioral and physical health, and needed a supervisor to train staff to work with those with mental health diagnoses, along with their other issues. Shazia applied for and acquired the job. Shazia also teaches, trains, and supervises family therapists as adjunct faculty.

What is most rewarding?

In her customer care supervisor job, Shazia notes, "I get to work with a talented group of individuals who contribute towards facilitation of care for the members. It can be as simple as finding a primary care physician for the member or as complex as finding someone to help them in the moment when they are going through a crisis. Also, seeing integrated care come to life in the real world is rewarding, where we are not only focusing on either physical health or behavioral health but are helping our members find physical and behavioral health resources simultaneously—in the belief there is no mind–body split—and that physical and behavioral health are mutually influencing processes."

What is most challenging?

Shazia had prior experience supervising and training clinicians, but supervising staff who do not have this background requires a different set of skills. She has found that "the rules of communication, for example, are different. I cannot assume that my staff knows the language of the healthcare system. I have to communicate with them on a fundamental level while maintaining the essence of information so that they can successfully deliver it to the members and providers. I also have to give them background information of how the healthcare system works, more specifically and clearly, so that it makes sense to them."

What about your MFT training is most helpful to you?

Shazia had training in medical family therapy (McDaniel, Doherty, & Hepworth, 2014), which she finds has been most useful to her. She adds, "I believe that biological and psychosocial-spiritual systems are interconnected and inter-dependent (each has an effect on the other) and that effective provision of healthcare services requires addressing issues of mind and body simultaneously. It was an easy transition for me because I am trained to recognize complexities and the interplay of multiple systems involved for individuals living with acute and chronic illnesses (biomedical, psychological, relational, sociocultural, spiritual, healthcare environments, etc.)—all systems are influencing and being influenced by each other. Therefore, as a systemic thinker, I felt comfortable when working with individuals, families, and physical and behavioral health providers towards facilitation of integrated care (and coordination of care for our members) while attending to variables of diversity including culture, age, gender, and sexuality in an empathic and respectful environment. This is what I do and teach my staff on a daily basis as a supervisor."

About diversity

Shazia's background gives her a unique focus on education as an avenue for creating opportunities for self and others. "I came to US as an international student to pursue an MS degree in MFT because acquiring education was considered very important to my family, especially my parents. My parents had motivated me to get higher education with assumptions that education leads to further opportunities and improved quality of life, especially for women in lesser developed parts of the world. This motivation stayed with me and after I attained my MS degree, and to further my education, I joined and completed the PhD program. While I was getting my doctoral degree, I made sure that I also worked on acquiring relevant professional credentials such as MFT licensure (LMFT) and certification as an addition professional (CAP). Attaining the degrees and the credentials did open up work opportunities for me and I am not sure if I would have had those opportunities without the credentials I have today (especially as an international student, for whom work permit requirements are different and rigorous). Both my parents are deceased now but their legacy lives on as I continue to look for opportunities to educate myself further (such as meeting requirements for Fellow in Thanatology). Believing in education as a key to opening up the door to future opportunities, I encourage the staff members I supervise at work to pursue higher education so they also have access to expanded career opportunities in their future."

FARIHA'S STORY

Fariha Niazi, Training Manager of Operations, Managed Care Company

Background

Fariha is a licensed marriage and family therapist, with both a master's and a doctoral degree. She is currently the Training Manager of Operations for a large managed care company.

What is this job like?

Fariha trains new hires and existing staff in the operations department of an integrated program. As she explains it, an integrated program is "a health plan that covers both physical and behavioral health for individuals living with serious mental health diagnoses including psychotic and depressive disorders." She trains both customer care and field operations staff. Customer care staff is nonclinical; field operations staff are mental health professionals, both licensed and nonlicensed, and nurses. She provides ongoing training to staff of both types.

How do you get a job like this?

Fariha started out working as an in-home family therapist for an agency, rising to the position of Regional Director. She left that position to work for her current company in utilization review. When this position opened up in supervision and training, she applied for it and was hired as a training manager.

What is most rewarding?

Fariha finds most rewarding "the relationships I establish with the staff. I train them but I am not their supervisor, so our interaction is not consistent on a daily basis, but my trainees come back to me after the training has ended and they have taken on their full responsibilities as employees, to tell me how well they are doing. They ask me if I am proud of them. I think the relationship with a trainer is a special one, because when new staff start, they spend most of their time in training with me. It is typically the very first relationship they develop at work. Training experience, in a respectful and trusting environment, stays with them and, at times, motivates them to do well. In addition, I like that I am using my training as an MFT in the context of managed care. It shows the wide applicability of family systems ideas in other contexts (other than in-room therapy or clinical supervision)."

What is most challenging?

Moving to this different context was challenging at first for Fariha. But she utilized her systems training and learned, "The context and rules of interactions (at workplace) may be different but the processes of how people relate to each other are similar."

What about your MFT training is most helpful to you?

The concepts of context and systems are important to Fariha. "In all human systems environments, including workplaces, my philosophy has been to work collaboratively with those involved and explore their strengths and resources to facilitate achievement of their goals (such as training goals) while remaining respectful to the differences. As a family therapist I have learned that behaviors, including learning, take place in a relational context, and paying attention to the context in which the behavior takes place is of utmost importance to understand the behavior (in the case of my work, the context is the training room). I believe that in any given context a person influences others and is influenced by others. Therefore, as a trainer, it is important to me to take as much time as needed to engage my trainees so that they can feel part of the process and can participate in a dynamic manner."

About diversity

Fariha notes, "When I started my journey as an MFT, I was an international student with English as my second language. Over the years, I have worked on becoming better at spoken and written English, which remains my second language. Today I train staff at work in English and the interesting aspect is that almost everyone I have trained is bilingual with English as their second language, although their first language is different than mine. So we have an interplay of several languages in the context of training: i.e., my first language, their first language, language of our dominant culture (English), language of our organization (terminologies and abbreviations specific to the workplace), and language of the healthcare system (different types of disorders, treatments, etc.). As we maneuver through our training, we have to work with all these languages and at times co-create a new language of our own (that may be unique to each one of us), combining all the languages (mentioned above), to be able to successfully do our jobs. For me as a trainer, I have learned to talk on a fundamental level: that is, without assuming what my trainees know and starting from the beginning of every topic I train them in. I have also realized that the effective use of tools of language, such as metaphors, questions, etc., are very powerful with regards to engaging and motivating my trainees. In addition, I have noticed that as they all come from different cultures, and even if they come from the same or similar cultures sometimes, they have different languages (verbal and nonverbal) to communicate with me and each other. I have worked on linking the verbal with nonverbal to be able to make sense of their learning behaviors in relation to that of my own. In other words, if someone is not making eye contact with me when I deliver information, I have realized that it does not mean that they are not learning—not making eye contact may have a different meaning in that trainee's culture than what I think it is, based on my cultural assumptions. I just have to be open to the behavior and explore what this behavior may mean and how it may impact the context of learning of the trainee and everyone involved in the context, including myself."

REFERENCE

McDaniel, S., Doherty, W., & Hepworth, J. (2014). *Medical family therapy: Integrated care* (2nd edn.). New York: APA.

Chapter 11

About University and Postgraduate Settings

Martha Gonzalez Marquez

Some marriage and family therapists choose to either work in full-time academia or to supplement their work with part-time teaching. From community colleges in departments such as human development to doctoral level and post-degree granting institutions, marriage and family therapists have expertise to share. Marriage and family therapists can teach in programs that cover areas related to our field, such as sociology, diversity, psychology, mental health, and social work, as well as teach in programs that focus on marriage and family therapy specifically. We can play other roles in educational settings as well, such as advisors and administrators. Their systemic expertise prepares them to counsel students seeking guidance and may also give them the exact tools needed to work in administrative positions. Additionally, with the increasing number of online programs, therapists have even more options open to them for teaching. We interview Rosario, who works for a university as an undergraduate student advisor; Iliàmaris (Ili), who teaches undergraduate counseling students via an online program while also running her own private practice; and Jacquie, who along with her coaching practice, teaches in a post-degree institution that specializes in marriage and family therapy.

OUR SUCCESS STORIES RECOMMEND . . .

Students are a special population, and sensitivity to their needs is important. Rosario notes that, as with clients, they can be led to knowledge, but not forced into it. All our success stories agree it is important to stay current in the field, and accommodate to the learning needs of diverse students. The importance of connecting with other professionals also cannot be overestimated. Ili states, "Don't hesitate to contact an acquaintance to express interest in a job opportunity. Professional growth is often based on personal connections." Jacquie's advice centers on a spiritual note: "I encourage graduates to examine and clarify how MFT training connects with your life purpose." Training and teaching and helping others to learn is rewarding for Rosario, Iliàmaris, and Jacquie.

ROSARIO'S STORY

Rosario Koenig, Academic Advisor, University Setting

Background

Rosario has a master's in family therapy. She is an Academic Advisor II, working at the Undergraduate Academic Advising Center of a large university.

What is this job like?

Rosario explains, "On a daily basis I have the opportunity and pleasure of working with individuals who want to earn an education to realize their dream of profitable career, aspirations, passions. As an advisor I provide guidance with their course work as well as through the processes of the university. I meet with the traditional day student, the continuing education student who transfers from another institution, the adult learner, and online students from various parts of the country.

"As an advisor I provide students with information on the field of study they choose to follow, with consideration of the careers goals they have in mind, while creating a relationship that encourages their connection to the university. Working through the transition of coming from high school or transferring in to complete their bachelor's, students must go through an adjustment period of learning the university culture. At the student's first meeting, the review of the major requirements and how to achieve the goal of graduation is discussed in a proactive manner."

How do you get a job like this?

Rosario applied to the university where she was obtaining her graduate degree in marriage and family therapy. She emphasized her relationship-building skills, and her ability to work with family members (anxious parents of undergraduates) as well as students themselves. The hiring committee appreciated her MFT skills and felt they were a good fit. Rosario initially started as a graduate advisor, but prefers working with undergraduates, as the relationships are longer term.

What is most rewarding?

Witnessing the growth and development of students, as they mature into confident adults, is very rewarding for Rosario.

What is most challenging?

Deadlines and paperwork can challenge both the students and Rosario. It is also a challenge to keep up with the latest resources and skills.

 92

What about your MFT training is most helpful to you?

Rosario notes, "The training I received in the Marriage and Family Therapy Program is very useful in working with students . . . I love advising in a systemic way to understand their career goals and engagement with clubs or associations in the university. Inevitably, I notice a mentor or situation that left an impression, or goals encouraged by family members. I have the opportunity, and pleasure, to facilitate students' transition from high school to college and, perhaps, graduate school. I am able to experience their growth. As a result, I find myself applying some key components from solution-focused, relational, MRI, narrative, collaborative language and other social constructionist models."

About diversity

"As an academic advisor, I love advising in a systemic way, making a difference with a diverse population. I have the opportunity to work with Saudi Arabians to Central and South Americans, as well as Europeans. I give credit to my own parents, who moved to the United States when I was five years old, and to becoming a naturalized citizen. As a first-generation, Latin American woman with ancestry from China and Inca Indian, raised Roman Catholic in the United States, I can identify the struggles of acculturation, work ethic, and the roles of men and women. I have a sense of responsibility and service to treat them with respect in introducing the American ways. I encourage education to women in general and to Hispanic women in particular, as I can relate to strict parental figures, for example. I intentionally position myself in situations to make a difference. I'm a member of the American Association of University Women, and I was recognized as the 'Student Organization Advisor of the Year' 2014 for AAUW student organization on campus. Our signature event is 'International Women's Day,' which celebrates the empowerment of all women, and men who support women, because that is how we got the vote!"

ILI'S STORY

Iliàmaris Rivera Walter, Adjunct Instructor and Private Practitioner

Background

Ili has a master's in family therapy. She is licensed in two states and is an AAMFT approved supervisor. In addition to her private practice, Ili teaches online as an adjunct instructor.

What is this job like?

Ili describes the role of an adjunct: "As an adjunct instructor, I hear student concerns via email and phone, and I help solve these concerns, while advocating for the student's progress with other systems with which he/she may be involved, such as practicum and internship sites. I also maintain and update online course content."

How did you get this job?

Regarding her teaching, Ili shares, "I was an undergraduate instructor for the department when I lived near the college's campus. While a doctoral student, I contacted the program director to discuss opportunities for teaching in the graduate program. I was offered the chance to teach one course that semester, and have been teaching at least two courses each semester since." Ili also explains about her practice. "For private practice, I always knew I wanted to be able to offer couples therapy in a private practice setting. I decided to start the practice while I was in the coursework portion of my doctoral studies, in order to focus on my studies and still be able to work part time."

What is most rewarding?

Ili reflects on the importance of the interpersonal nature of her work. "I like having conversations with people. I enjoy hearing others' perspectives, as well as helping them recognize their perspectives and needs. I appreciate being able to witness the connection that happens between people when they finally understand each other, or are finally able to put a behavior in context."

What is most challenging?

Ili states, "Sometimes, it's difficult seeing the long-term impact of your work. I think there are several reasons for this, including the need for me as a therapist to be focused on the current session. Even with the full picture of a client's past and current therapy work, therapists don't always see the long-term impact of their work on clients' lives. Being in private practice can also be difficult for having a sense of how day-to-day responsibilities contribute to career development. In other words, unless a solo practitioner wants to develop into a group practice, there isn't a clear progression from direct service to supervisory/management responsibilities, which can be more easily delineated by working for an agency or in other settings. Ili reflects, "Because I work as an online adjunct instructor, I am held to expectations regarding contact to which a traditional instructor (on-campus) might not have to adhere. Beyond those expectations, I have learned that it is essential that I check in with students via email and announcements on a regular

 94

basis, so they see me not only as an active instructor, but as someone who is concerned with their overall progress. This means that I view my position as an online instructor as an on-call position. There is no guideline to when students can contact me; I do, however, keep a schedule for myself. I think the challenge is balancing great customer service with reasonable boundaries for the work."

What about your MFT training is most helpful to you?

Ili shares about the impact of her MFT training: "My family therapy training has made me who I am. It has profoundly shaped my worldview, my view of relational interactions, as well as my relationship with self. In day-to-day work, my training allows me to genuinely interact and connect with others and accurately assess and treat clients presenting problems. In addition, my training contributes to a level of sensitivity regarding the interpretation of communication in professional and personal circles, the evaluation of boundaries, and my own and others' emotional reactions."

About diversity

Ili shares her perspective on diversity. "The main aspects of my culture that influence my work are regarding my personal multicultural experiences. I am Latina, but I also had the opportunity to live in other countries during my childhood. This exposure helped me understand how culture influences individuals' preferences. I believe that I am able to see cultural aspects of relating that, perhaps, an LMFT with less exposure to other nationalities would not see as clearly. In addition, I identify as Christian, and this is the lens through which I assimilate information. Therefore, my chosen theories, policies, and ways of working align not only with the AAMFT ethical code, but also with my views about my responsibility to fellow human beings.

"Because I specialize in working with couples, and they are mainly heterosexual, I am very aware of my gender as a female. I am cognizant of my role in joining with both the male and female partner, and I talk with my clients about my views on joining and multidirectional partiality. Before moving to South Florida, I lived and practiced in central Pennsylvania. The main cultural factor influencing my work and bringing in clients was my faith. Once I began my practice in South Florida, a very diverse community, my clients mainly included interracial and interethnic couples and Spanish-speaking clients, along with ethnically diverse clients and couples who identified as Christian, and chose me for this affiliation."

In addition, she tells us, "Because I offer a sliding scale, I have been able to work with clients and couples of varying socioeconomic status. I believe that my work with culturally diverse populations helps to keep me innovative as a therapist and contributes to my love of this work."

JACQUIE'S STORY

Jacqueline (Jacquie) Braeger, Assistant Professor, Executive Life Coach

Background

Jacquie has a doctoral degree in family therapy, is licensed, is an AAMFT Approved Supervisor, and is iPEC certified in Executive and Life Coaching as well as in iPEC Energy Leadership. She is currently teaching at a post-degree, COAMFTE Accredited MFT, faith-based institution. Jacquie has held multiple positions in the behavioral service delivery system for over 30 years including military systems, community mental health, secondary school corporations, hospital systems, home based services, undergraduate and graduate institutions.

What is this job like?

After a morning of personal and family routine, Jacquie heads to the institution and "begins work which consists of supervising students, facilitating practicum groups, designing curriculum, mentoring/advising students, attending committee meetings, assisting the Admissions Office with student recruitment requests, preparing for class, teaching (usually one course per semester . . . sometimes two courses), seeing a small amount of private clients for therapy, coaching or supervision, and collaborating with various colleagues on presentations and writing projects." She shares that her current academic position is 24 hours per week part-time and she also earns additional pay for extra courses and supervision. Including her coaching, Jacquie totals 35–40-hour work week. She states, "I try to keep Friday open for self-care, nurturing relationships, and professional projects of my choosing."

How do you get a job like this?

"I was recruited by a fellow graduate student (who was also an ordained Lutheran minister and had been hired as an assistant professor at the institution) to teach a graduate MFT class as she was leaving for a spouse's job opportunity in another state." Jacquie describes her path as having begun teaching one course, then supervising in their residency program, then supervising in a practicum. She then began teaching courses every semester. Jacquie became an affiliate professor in 2007, and then an Assistant Professor in 2014.

What is most rewarding?

"Every day I wake up excited to go to work. I am passionate about the work I do! And while I work hard, it feels energizing and life transforming. It feels like I am making a real difference in people's lives, fulfilling a spiritual calling, a higher life purpose. I have the sense that I am creatively utilizing my greatest strengths in the service of the greater good, promoting everyone's highest flourishing! On a pragmatic level, I really appreciate the flexibility of this work. I can create my own schedule and work rhythm, which has been key in partnering with my spouse in raising our four children and supporting a core focus on life balance. I see relationship as central, and strive to privilege a lifestyle that supports the nourishing of self in relationship with others. I also appreciate the entrepreneurial spirit of this work, and the ways in which I have been able to contract with multiple funding streams in order to earn a sustainable income."

What is most challenging?

Jacquie shares, "I have had to educate professionals and consumers about the value of systemic work. My experience has been that once exposed to this, people really become excited about the results of working systemically. I have cultivated an entrepreneurial mindset in doing this work, particularly as it relates to earning a living. If you want to fit into a ready-made job description, and do not want to manage the anxiety that accompanies the uncertainty of crafting your own career path, this may feel more challenging! I would rather do work that aligns with my own sense of authenticity, where I work from my core strengths in the service of creative transformation, than fit a certain job category/description that is predetermined and restrictive."

What about your MFT training is most helpful to you?

"I am currently employed as an assistant professor of MFT, so all aspects of my MFT training are utilized. I teach MFT theory and systemic conceptualization, clinically supervise practicum students, develop course curriculum, and mentor students in their ongoing professional development. In addition, I consult with a variety of professionals who seek support in learning and applying a family systems perspective in their work. For example, psychologists have sought guidance on child and adolescent cases, pastors with congregational group dynamics, and corporations with stress-management and health promotion education. I also incorporate my MFT training in my professional development coaching work. I believe this has given me a desired perspective that sets my work apart from a mainstream approach to these areas of intervention. I also contract with clinical graduates seeking supervision in working toward state licensure in MFT, and work with clients seeking relational counseling."

97

About diversity

Jacquie states, "Social location has played a predominant role in my professional experience. As a female professional, I have often experienced myself as marginalized and invisible when it came to power structure within organizations. Since I have worked a series of part-time and contract work, I have been a system outlier . . . working on the professional margins, so to speak. Given my own experiences with invisibility, I have a heart for those experiencing marginalization, and seek to empower students, supervisees and clients to find and utilize their authentic voices. I have also been fortunate to work with a rich diversity of people. The military system was my first encounter with major diversity regarding race, ethnicity/nationality, class and religious diversity. I was fortunate to be working with a system 30 years ago on the cutting edge of valuing and maximizing work performance through diversity. In addition, I currently work in a system that privileges and values diversity, including racial, ethnic, gender, religious, and age diversity; 40 percent of our students are people of color. We are an ecumenical seminary where diverse faith perspectives (including atheists and agnostic) are valued and respected. And students of all ages (from 22 years through retirement age) work and learn together."

Chapter 12

About Faith-Based Settings

Anne Rambo

Faith-based settings may be a good fit for those marriage and family therapists with strong religious convictions. The relational focus of marriage and family therapy makes this approach especially suited to combine with specific religious teachings about marriage, child rearing, family values, and relating to others. Typically, marriage and family therapists in faith-based settings may work with children, in religious schools, or as counselors/marriage educators with couples. Licensure is often preferred, but state regulations may exempt faith-based settings from professional regulations, allowing the hiring of otherwise qualified, and unlicensed practitioners. Salary ranges are similar to other school-based positions for religious schools (as this is typically a school-based position), to private nonprofit agency salaries for agencies (such as Jewish Family Services), and to private practice for work with couples (as this work may often depend on couples paying for services such as therapy and workshops, under the auspices of the religious organization). Examples follow from Jewish (Patti), Protestant Christian (Leslie and Simone), Catholic Christian (Bobbi), and Muslim (Amnah) settings.

OUR SUCCESS STORIES RECOMMEND . . .

It is important to communicate with your faith community all along, throughout your training and while working at other jobs in the field. Let the leaders within your community know that you want to use your professional skills to serve and minister. Identify major issues for your community, perhaps including divorce, family conflict, and children in need of religious instruction, and offer programs targeted to these needs.

PATTI'S STORY

Patti Sinkoe, Director of Behavioral Health, Goodman Jewish Family Service Agency

Background

Patti is the Director of Behavioral Health for a large Jewish social services agency. Her agency offers individual, couple, and family counseling services, support groups, domestic abuse services, a special outreach to elderly Holocaust survivors, and many other programs. Unless designated for a special population, the programs are open to the general public, regardless of faith. Patti is a licensed marriage and family therapist.

What is this job like?

Patti is responsible for overseeing intakes and assessments, supervising clinicians, and handling any client concerns. She also carries a small clinical caseload of her own. She is moving her agency to electronic record keeping, which involves both setting up systems and training staff. In addition, she and her staff collaborate with other agencies in the Jewish community, for example offering groups at the JCC, and providing counseling for athletes participating in the Maccabee games. Finally, she participates in community outreach, spreading the word about the programs her agency offers.

How do you get a job like this?

Patti recommends choosing an internship which will give you relevant experience. She interned at Jewish Family Services, and got to know the agency well, volunteering to participate in agency-sponsored events and taking an interest in all agency programs. After graduation, she worked for this same Jewish Family Services agency first as an intake coordinator, and then as a case manager for elderly Holocaust survivors. Once licensed, she worked briefly in managed care, which she credits as teaching her much about record keeping. But she wanted to go back to the agency she calls "home," and accepted their offer when a directorship became available.

What is most rewarding?

Patti finds it rewarding to know she is making a difference every day. It is also rewarding to her that her personal convictions and values reinforce the work that she does. Patti is especially proud to have launched Project DASH—Dental Assistance Services for Survivors of the Holocaust, a program providing pro bono dental care for needy Holocaust survivors in the community.

What is most challenging?

It is challenging for Patti when her agency cannot help someone in the community, either because resources are insufficient or the type of help the client wants is not possible. She tries her best to turn no client away.

What about your MFT training is most helpful to you?

Patti stresses the importance of systemic thinking, and sensitivity to cultural difference. She has found it important to consider the whole system, rather than just partition off mental health and deal only with that. For example, when she was working with elderly Holocaust survivors, getting them funded for necessary medical care was an important part of her job, and rewarding to her.

About diversity

Patti describes her agency as "guided by Jewish values, but serving the entire community." As she puts it, "We do what we do because we are Jewish—not because we're serving only the Jewish population. We are serving everyone, from a base of Jewish values." Feeling connected to a community in which she has deep roots is rewarding to her.

LESLIE'S STORY

Leslie Griffin, Protestant Christian Family Life Educator

Background

Leslie has a master's in marriage and family therapy, and has also obtained a doctorate in family studies, qualifying her as a family life educator. Her passion is revitalizing marriages from within the Protestant Christian perspective.

What is this job like?

Leslie currently serves as the coordinator of counseling for a large church. She founded a private nonprofit organization called Christian C.O.O.P.S. of America—the acronym stands for Couples Offering One Another Prayer and Support. In addition, she has established Marriage Champs LLC to further present her work with couples. She is at work on a book, titled *State of the Union: Addressing the Marriage Crisis in the Christian Church*, and has a blog, "W.I.S.E. talk with Dr. Leslie Griffin." She also presents widely as a motivational speaker.

101

How do you get a job like this?

Leslie describes herself as a creative person and an entrepreneur. She worked in the field for a private nonprofit agency immediately after graduation with her master's, and then went on to doctoral study in the area of family life education. She stayed active in her church and with outreach to couples, but felt something was missing with existing programs. As she puts it, "I'm a fairly creative person, which means I'm constantly thinking of innovative ways to meet the needs of my target population. I've come across hundreds of programs and services aimed at helping couples successfully navigate marriage, but I could not find anything that captured the essence of marriage as I saw it. In addition, I could not find anything that I believed would be fun and engaging for men. Consequently, with the help of my husband, I created it."

What is most rewarding?

Leslie comments, "Counseling in a faith-based setting works for me because it gives me an automatic strength to work with. It helps me identify with the client, fosters a connection and facilitates the joining process which I think is so important." Leslie also enjoys the opportunity to be a source of encouragement and support.

What is most challenging?

Initially, Leslie struggled with finding her own therapeutic identity—finding a model that worked for her, and reaching out to prospective clients with a clear message about what she can offer that is unique. Now that she is well on her way towards that goal, she is still challenged, as are most therapists, by discouraging cases and the need for self-care.

What about your MFT training is most helpful to you?

Reflecting, Leslie identifies, "The two things that have resonated most and make me good at what I do are (1) the idea that all behaviors make sense in context, and (2) that problems are only problems in relationship to others." This systemic thinking she credits as foundational to her success. She advises other beginning marriage and family therapists to trust their unique gift.

About diversity

"I am a 36-year-old, middle-class, African-American, heterosexual, married woman. Working as a therapist in a faith-based setting fits who I am and what I believe about people and the world in which we live. Demographics are really not important in a faith-based environment. What matters is that every client feels respected, supported and accepted."

SIMONE'S STORY

Simone Finnis, Former director of a Protestant Christian family ministry, and private practice

Background

Simone is a licensed marriage and family therapist, with a private practice with a strong spiritual orientation. Having been the Director of Family and Ministry Services for a large non-denominational Christian church, she moved into her therapy practice to offer additional services in this area.

What is this job like?

Simone integrates complementary methods such as prayer, meditation, and mindfulness, along with evidence-based therapies such as solution-focused brief therapy and structural family therapy. She explains, "Clients who seek out my services are looking for a highly tailored effective approach that meets their and their loved ones' unique needs."

How do you get a job like this?

Simone studied to become a marriage and family therapist after years in the ministry, and draws on that experience in her work.

What is most rewarding?

Simone bubbles with enthusiasm. "Really just seeing clients achieve their goals and experience transformation and change. A lot of times people come in with what they feel are insurmountable obstacles, and they feel disempowered or like they don't deserve a better life or that they can't achieve what they are seeking. That process of reaching out for help, seeing them achieve what they thought was impossible, is pretty incredible. It's amazing to me every single time. Sometimes I even say to the clients, 'This is beautiful!' "

What is most challenging?

It has been challenging for Simone to move from being a registered intern to a licensed practitioner, and accept her own professional value. As she notes, "I had

103

to challenge myself to raise my rates and value myself as was consistent with the market. I am more comfortable with this now."

What about your MFT training is most helpful to you?

The systemic approach is a fit with Simone's relational values and she has found it works well with a variety of presenting problems. She also uses a variety of family therapy approaches including solution-focused, structural, intergenerational, and narrative models. She finds relational thinking and values an excellent fit with her approach.

About diversity

Simone has a multicultural background, with multiple different ethnic identifications—"at least five." She finds this helps her with couples who are experiencing intermarriage difficulties. In addition, she feels diverse clients who may have felt marginalized by other therapists tend to gravitate to her. Many of her clients are also drawn to working with someone with a Christian background—"they have different anchors in their belief systems which I can tap into to increase their resilience."

BOBBI'S STORY

Bobbi,* Catholic School-Based Counselor

Background

Bobbi is a school counselor in a private Catholic school. She has her master's in family therapy and obtained a school social worker certification and thus a certification as a guidance counselor is not necessary in her setting. She is also a certified ScreamFree Parenting Facilitator.

What is this job like?

Bobbi explains, "I see students for individual short-term counseling . . . mostly family—divorce concerns/peer relations/educational or social skills. I work with students who may be having behavior problems (although I work at a private Catholic school and our behavior issues are not very severe).

* Last name has been withheld by request.

"I work with students to set up goals and plans (educational and behavioral). Students respond well to looking at exceptions to their problem behaviors. Students will stop by my office as needed. No need for appointments." Bobbi also works with parents, runs groups, and provides classroom lessons in social skills areas. She works with exceptional student education plans, and coordinates assessments. As she notes, "Every day is different. Which is great—it all depends what students, administrators, or teachers need from me."

How do you get a job like this?

Bobbi was working for a private Catholic school as the registrar when she went back to school for her graduate degree. She was then hired as a counselor. Since then she has worked in other area Catholic schools. She states it is important to know and be known in the community of the Catholic school system.

What is most rewarding?

Bobbi feels she may often not know how influential she was until after the fact. She tells the story: "It's rewarding to be doing something that may seem insignificant to me but makes a powerful change in someone's life. A few years ago a student graduated 8th grade and gave me a letter. Her letter talked about how I helped her when she was in 6th grade with a peer problem. She elaborated on how my help and support really changed her thoughts about herself and her friendships. The thing that struck me the most was how I could not even remember the situation. I just hope that I can make a difference just by being there. Someone they can turn to and trust."

What is most challenging?

At times Bobbi finds her faith-based setting constraining. This is particularly true when it comes to sexuality issues. As she describes, "In the past ten years I have run into conflicts in working with students who are struggling with their sexuality. One instance was when two 8th grade girls were kissing in the bathroom. The girls were referred to me—this was difficult because I knew that I had to take the approach of the Church and what I really wanted to do was explore further with the girls."

What about your MFT training is most helpful to you?

Bobbi cites the solution-focused approach she learned in her master's program as pivotal to her work. She describes, "I attempt to always use 'solution language' when speaking with teachers regarding a student. They come to me expecting me to give them a magic solution. When in fact with a little talk they will realize they already have the solution. I feel my job is to advocate for the student and to do this successfully I do need to have the faculty buy in as well . . . I am fortunate to have a wonderful partner in the ESE teacher. I have even had her read the RTI solution-focused book and she has adopted the philosophy."

About diversity

Bobbi comments, "I tend to have more liberal views then most of my colleagues. So balancing my political and social believes within the confines of my work environment is sometimes a challenge. I have usually handled this by not commenting on current topics; for example, I did not keep my Obama bumper sticker on my work car. Also this means not discussing my views with students, which is the down side." Overall, though, she finds the rewards of working in a faith-based setting are worth the conflicts for her. "It really does make us all (faculty, admin, and students) a community. We share our faith through daily prayer and a weekly 'interactive' student Mass. Our school motto is a quote that sums up our community perfectly: 'Preach the Gospel every day and if necessary use words.'"

AMNAH'S STORY

Amnah Alenazi, Marital Educator in Mosque Settings

Background

Amnah has a master's in family therapy and is currently studying for her doctorate in family therapy in the United States. She resides permanently in Saudi Arabia. Here in the United States, she presents workshops to area mosques on marital issues.

What is this job like?

Amnah is translating a book on family therapy into Arabic. She has presented at several United States mosques on solution-focused approaches to marital conflict, and is scheduled for similar workshops in Dubai and Kuwait. Her audiences are married women. Her goal is to empower women to overcome marital and other challenges.

How do you get a job like this?

Amnah volunteered her initial workshops to get experience and to become known in this area. She also has contacts in the faith community, as well as training in marital education and solution-focused coaching.

What is most rewarding?

Amnah states, "The most rewarding to me is definitely that I develop professionally and get more skills. Honestly another thing that I will never forget it is when I became a different person who sees things differently and thinks systemically."

What is most challenging?

Building bridges between her home country and the United States, and between her faith community and others outside that context, has been challenging but important for Amnah.

What about your MFT training is the most helpful to you?

Amnah feels her family therapy training "is not just about helping my clients to overcome their problems; it also assists me as a therapist and mother in many aspects in my life. Systemically I learned how important it is to know that one member of the family can affect others, so it is significant to get better understanding about family relationships. I also learned how important it is for therapists to be more effective and work collaboratively in session with clients by spending time to build a good relationship with them. Indeed, family therapy training provides different approaches to pick up what you feel comfortable using with your client and truly match your personal style."

About diversity

Amnah is a young 30-year-old married woman and mother who wears the hijab and dresses conservatively. As she notes, "Throughout my education and especially in my practical training I faced many challenges because of my religion, gender, and ethnicity. Some people resisted to talk to me because of my hijab or my accent and so on. My biggest challenges came when I worked in a public school setting seeing teens and kids. Once I remember my supervisor allowed me and my colleagues to each select one of the students and start a session. So, I come close to an African-American boy to talk with him, but he refused to go with me, then I told myself OK, maybe he is not in a good mood, so I went to the next student, who sat next to him. The other student said, 'No, I do not want talk to you because you are from the Middle East!!' I was shocked and I told myself I should talk with him to know why he said that and what he knows about Middle Eastern people. Many questions came out in my mind. Then, I sat down with him and talked about what makes him afraid of talking to me. It was a very interesting conversation and a great session. So, my advice is to not make a hurried judgment, especially with kids or teens, and keep in mind how social media has a huge impact in their life." Amnah feels such experiences will help her assist her workshop participants build bridges to others as well. As she notes, "The most important thing is that you need to love what you do and be patient and passionate to fulfill your dream and goals."

Chapter 13

About Indian Health Services and Related Settings

Tommie V. Boyd

The Federal Indian Health Services actively seeks marriage and family therapists to serve Native American tribes in underserved areas. There are four career paths available: civil service, direct tribal hire, USPHS commissioned corps, and (for veterans) military transition. Details of each are available at www.ihs.org.

The Indian Health Service will assign you to the tribal area which is the best fit for their needs and for yours—if you are seeking repayment of your student loans, this must be a designated loan-repayment site. Loan repayment is available at the rate of $20,000 per year in these designated sites. Similar arrangements are available through the National Health Service Corps—this is for rural and underserved areas, not necessarily tribal in nature (www.nhsc.hrsa.gov). Individual Native American tribes also separately fund positions, and these offer public service loan forgiveness like any other nonprofit or government entity (after ten years). Tribal settings offer, as well, a chance to immerse oneself in a different culture and learn from the experience. The locations are often beautiful and unique, and the clients welcoming. Marriage and family therapists seeking these opportunities should be aware, however, that locations in some cases may also be remote and somewhat isolated. Cultural humility is required above all—approach with curiosity, respect, and caution, mindful of the painful history with outsiders many Native American tribes have experienced. Licensure is required for federal programs, but may not be by individual Tribes.

OUR SUCCESS STORIES RECOMMEND . . .

Embrace the culture and attend tribal events (not just the ones directly related to your job). Learn all you can and be open to new experiences. Come prepared, with a wide range of varied clinical experiences. Stay humble and respectful, and think in relationship terms.

BRYAN'S STORY

Bryan Granie, Assistant Director, Seminole Tribe

Background

Bryan is the Assistant Director of Operations and Development for the Boys and Girls Clubs of the Seminole Tribe of Florida (BGC/STOF).

What is this job like?

Bryan oversees the Youth Development Program, and supervises the counseling provided by Youth Development Specialists. He also provides counseling as needed. He develops curriculum and trains staff on relevant developmental issues, such as behavior intervention, school problems, making friends, and so on.

How do you get a job like this?

Bryan feels it was important that people got to know him over time. He started with the Tribe as a part-time music instructor then transitioned into counseling as a Youth Development Specialist after graduating with his master's. After four years, he was promoted to his current position.

What is most rewarding?

Bryan is enthusiastic about his work. "The most rewarding thing about my job is the ability to witness the positive change and development in each youth that walks through the Club's door. Through the support of the Tribal Council and Community the BGC/STOF has been able to create a safe, positive environment where youth can excel in the following five core Boys and Girls Clubs of America (BGCA) program areas: character and leadership, education and career, health and life skills, the arts, and sports, fitness, and recreation. The goal is to create independent and productive contributors to society.

"Additionally, being able to witness the progress of the Youth Development Program has been extremely rewarding. This program is designed to provide special needs youth with systemically based and community oriented services to ensure their positive development within the Clubs. Additionally, it is designed to monitor and track the overall goals and development of every registered member within the BGC/STOF."

What is most challenging?

Bryan does not see any challenges other than expansion. He would like to bring systemic programming to Native youth programs across the country.

What about your MFT training is most useful to you?

Bryan identifies systemic thinking, and the ability to consider relationships in everything he does, as central to his success.

About diversity

Bryan notes, "I am male, Caucasian. I recently discovered that I have Delaware Indian in my blood, which has been pretty cool figuring out who exactly my ancestors are. I actually ran into some Delaware Tribal members at a recent conference which was interesting. I don't see my race or cultural identity affecting what I do, it's more of my ability to be culturally sensitive that affects what I do. Being able to understand the Seminole community and Native communities in general starts with respecting the history and traditions of the community as a whole. Approaching a diverse population with respect is the first step in creating a systemic framework around the work that you do with them. Additionally, you have to truly care about the people you serve and be genuinely invested in the well-being and future successes of every person in that community."

HOLLY'S STORY

Holly Carbone, Team Supervisor, White Mountain Apache

Background

Holly is a licensed marriage and family therapist. She has a master's and a doctoral degree in the field. She is the Child, Adolescent and Family Team Supervisor at Apache Behavioral Health Services, Inc. (ABHS).

What is this job like?

Holly comments, "One of the greatest benefits of my job is that I never have the same day twice. Working in a Tribal community means being flexible and that is this job. The ABHS Family Team has therapists in the office, schools, and community. We provide individual, family, and group therapy, as well as culturally relevant therapeutic programs. My day consists of program development, clinical supervision, crisis interventions, trainings, and anything else that needs to get done."

How do you get a job like this?

After experience in hospital and community-based settings, practicing medical family therapy, Holly applied to a job with the Apache through AAMFT's Job Connections page online. She was attracted to the loan forgiveness program, but has stayed due to the intangible rewards of the position. She recommends that those interested in family therapy positions with Native American Tribes do their homework in advance. "If new graduates want to work in Native communities, I would suggest spending time researching the cultures, as well as historical trauma. Maria Bravehart has provided a lot of wonderful information regarding historical trauma and published a great deal. Also, Maria Bigfoot has done some amazing work with native communities and trauma. Another aspect in researching native cultures is that there are over 500 registered tribal communities in the United States, each having its own values, beliefs and traditions. Understanding, as much as possible, what is important to the community can help with working with tribal members. In addition, be open to learning tradition and nontraditional ways of healing and communicating. Some of the ABHS Family Team staff recently worked with a teen group that we took to work in a river respiration project. The teens learned more about change and healing from the river then they would ever learn in talk therapy. The teens commented that as they helped to heal the river, they felt a healing within themselves. It provided an opportunity for the teens to provide a service to Mother Earth and feel connected to the land of their ancestors. This experience was profound and meaningful for the teens."

What is most rewarding?

Holly states that "being a guest and allowed to serve families in a Native American community is the most incredible experience of my life. It is humbling to be immersed in a culture that is so different from my own. Every day I am challenged to think of life experiences differently, and view community from a more expansive lens. The incredibly talented Tribal Members that I work with have taught me so much about the healing power of faith, connections, and community."

What is most challenging?

"Working on a reservation can be difficult if therapists are not getting out into the community to experience the strength, resilience, and joy of the Tribe," Holly notes. "We work with kids and families who experience multiple traumas, substance use/abuse, and suicide (just to name a few). Anyone working in communities with these really tough issues has to find a balance and see that there is much more to Tribal members then trauma, loss and sorrow. We (outsiders) have to also see, and experience, the incredible dedication to family, community, and traditions that provide the strength people need to work through hard times."

What about your MFT training is most helpful to you?

Holly gives an example to illustrate this point. "There isn't a day that goes by that I am not thankful for my marriage and family therapy training! Last month I had the honor of attending a Sunrise Dance, which is a rite-of-passage ceremony for young women. As I watched a strong young woman dance in the heat of the sun, backed by her Godparents and the medicine man, I was struck by deep value that is placed on community and family. Surrounding the inner group were extended family and community members who will support this young woman throughout her life. This ceremony was such a beautiful way to experience that an individual does not live in isolation but rather interconnected within systems. When the girl started getting tired, the community cheered her on, calling out to her that she wasn't alone and that she could get through. Her friends and family shouted to her that she was strong and she had the strength of her ancestors behind her, helping her on her journey. This experience reminded me of how we engage systems in a healing journey in therapy."

About diversity

Holly has thought long and hard about diversity within her present context. "It is both challenging and rewarding to work within a culture and community in which I was not raised. I cannot completely rely on my experience and education to invite clients into a place of change and growth. I have to continually be open to the many things that I 'don't know that I don't know.' This can be challenging because what I might consider therapeutic may not fit within the culture. I also do not know the language. A few years ago, when working with a Healing Circle (group for grief and loss), I quickly found that I had to sit quietly and just listen to the Apache language, rather than 'facilitate a group.' There are words in the Apache language that are far more descriptive to the devastation felt due to the death of a loved one and these words do not translate into English. At times, I feel limited by being an 'outsider,' but I *have* to be comfortable with these limitations in order to find other opportunities where I can connect."

SAMANTHA'S STORY

Samantha Corrington, Registered Clinical Counselor, Penelakut Tribe, Canada

Background

Samantha is a Registered Clinical Counselor in Ladysmith, British Columbia, Canada. She has a master's in MFT and an undergraduate degree in Child and

Youth Care. She is a clinical counselor who is contracted directly with the band and serves members of the Penelakut Tribe or community members living on the island. Penelakut Island is off the coast of Chemainus, BC, on Vancouver Island and can be accessed only be ferry or boat. It is also the location of the former Kuper Island Residential School.

What is this job like?

Samantha explains, "This job requires 'growing moss.' I need to sit still and show that I am not going to abandon the community. Community members pay very close attention to the comings and goings of outsiders, particularly settlers offering 'help.' Sometimes I have many clients, and other times there are few formal clients. I must be flexible and see my 'work' as being present in the community. The 'work' happens in line for the ferry, walking to the health unit, or sometimes just sitting on the couch in the reception area. This job is about serving the community. Whatever they need and following their lead in what that looks like. I must be very intuitive and often work with little direction, culturally and otherwise. I am very aware and respectful of working alongside of cultural traditional practices and try to gage when to be more invisible or silent.

"The Penelakut community, along with many aboriginal communities, is distrustful of the 'white' system and of the ongoing colonization that continues to impact community members. As much as I would like to pretend I am somehow different, I recognize that I do represent this system to many and am implicated in the current and historical transgressions and atrocities committed against First Nations peoples. I always remember being privy to an email which said 'I hope she doesn't plan to swoop in gun's a-blazing to fix all of our problems.' "

How do you get a job like this?

Samantha explains, "I was invited to serve the community after the suicide of a respected elder in the community. Through a professional relationship with the local Victim Services Program Manager I was introduced to the man who is now my supervisor and I am honored to call my big brother. At that time he was the Addictions Counselor; he is now the Health Unit Manager and a council member of the Tribe. I also met with various community members and members of the local Intertribal Health Authority, the agency responsible for the mental health services to the Tribe at the time. This vetting process took a few months as they consulted on my 'fit' within the community. I was initially tasked with short-term crisis counseling but was then invited to stay on. I went from one to two days a week at the request of the unit manager of the health center.

"After three years I am often asked what it is about me that 'fits' in this community. I am never sure just how to answer this. I do not impose my will.

I do not judge or pretend that I am an expert. I listen. I slow down. I just try to be authentic. And when I need help I seek it out."

What is most rewarding?

"What is most rewarding is feeling that, even as a white outsider, in many ways there is a sense of belonging . . . that I am theirs. The community has taken ownership of me in their own way. The stories and experiences that many members have had at the hands of the Canadian government and the churches that ran the residential school humble me. That people feel comfortable sharing this with me and if our work together brings them a sense of peace or hope in any way, 'there is no greater gift'."

What is most challenging?

"Ensuring I am aware of how I am implicated in the colonization of aboriginal people. Not convincing myself that I am somehow different than every other white settler. Owning and being aware of when I am taking up more space than I should and reminding myself to slow down. And when I let the language of colonizing systems (intergenerational violence, deep trauma, and systemic substance abuse) impact my confidence in what I can offer and impact the lens through which I view my clients. Challenging my own values, beliefs, and biases and attempting to create spaces and experiences of decolonized practice. Ensuring I am an ally not just when I am 'with a client' but in my own personal world."

What about your MFT training is most helpful to you?

"The value and importance of seeking out appropriate supervision. Technically, being in private practice I could easily work in a bubble. But I value the importance of supervision; supervision that challenges and pushes me. That allows me to be honest and sit in my own discomfort. I am developing a team of supervision. Individuals in the field who have differing views that push me in different ways that remind me of different ways I live my ethics.

"I seem to have developed a natural systems lens. I see all people within systems and even though I often only work with an individual, I am constantly looking at the impact of various systems and the importance of them in my clients' lived experience. I tend not to see the client as the problem but the problem as the problem.

"I also am thankful for my MFT training that helped me build my own way of working with clients. I bring myself to the process. I am playful yet respectful, which seems to work very well for me, and hopefully, my clients."

115

About diversity

Samantha states, "I try to be aware of my own curiosity. I am completely and utterly fascinated with the traditional cultural practices of the Coast Salish peoples, and the Penelakut Tribe specifically. I need to ensure that my own need to know or interest does not lead to me intruding on my clients. An example of this was working with a client and asking questions about her upcoming naming ceremony. At one point I noticed she had physically withdrawn from me and I asked what I was missing. 'It is not my place to tell you and it is not your place to know.' I try to remember this in my work. Every family and the work of their family is different. It is not always mine to know."

Chapter 14

About Corporate Settings and Entrepreneurial Work

Martha Gonzalez Marquez

Marriage and family therapists are systemic therapists, with expertise in how relationships between and among individuals in any system influence behavior. This expertise is valuable in not only the therapy setting, but also in organizations, corporate settings, as well as in product development. Many roles within an organization exist for systems therapists although their title may not reflect it. Marriage and family therapists are also in a unique position to create positions that organizations or corporations may benefit from. The marriage and family therapy emphasis on cultural diversity also provides preparation for work in diversity training within organizations. Most often, marriage and family therapists enter a corporate system through utilization review or human resources, but once in the system, their role may expand and change. Opening one's own business consulting to corporations in the areas of relationship building and diversity is another path, as is developing products from systemic perspectives. Typically, corporate salaries are higher than those in the private nonprofit field, but this may differ widely with each employment position. Being an entrepreneur also carries with it similar benefits as private practice with its flexibility, creativity, and independence.

OUR SUCCESS STORIES RECOMMEND . . .

One strong message—be creative and think outside the box. We interviewed Marilyn, a corporate consultant, who advises, "Broaden your thinking about systems to include the application of family therapy to family businesses that may need consulting with the overlay of a family history running the business. Also consider diversity, and the elements affected by diversity." Jodi, a senior director in a major corporation, adds, "Be true to yourself—this is like a marriage. Find a company that completes you and you complete it. Find a job that makes you a better professional." She goes on and shares, "Be curious. Never assume you have all the answers; question all answers and help people to see that there are a number of different ways to approach each problem; build a reputation as someone who is a systemic thinker and who has the managerial courage to admit when you don't have all the answers or make a mistake; help people to see you as someone who learns from those mistakes and rises up with even better solutions because of it." Jodi also shares the importance of learning the company's language and not over-defining your career path, and Avi, an entrepreneur, recommends seeing a need, and taking a risk to meet that need.

MARILYN'S STORY

Marilyn Nagel, Corporate Co-Founder Consultant

Background

Marilyn is CEO of Ready-Aim-Aspire, and Co-Founder and Chief Mission Officer of NQuotient. "NQuotient is a cloud-based networking tool that helps women to accelerate their career advancement and success. This Ready-Aim-Aspire company is a proprietary coaching method that assists clients in accomplishing their goals and heightening their presence."

What is this job like?

For Ready-Aim-Aspire, Marilyn has individual coaching clients, whom she meets with for 90-minute sessions with 20-minute check-in calls between sessions. She also delivers workshops and speaks at conferences and corporate events. For NQuotient, she has calls with prospective companies who want to pilot the product, works on product development and training material development, and meets with potential and current investors, the company's blog writer, the CEO, and consultants to the project. Marilyn blogs regularly and does interviews with news media.

How do you get a job like this?

Marilyn came to this position from a career in diversity training and nonprofit administration. She explains, "I created my company Ready-Aim-Aspire after retiring from running a large nonprofit. I was asked to join the NQuotient team because of my work in networking and its impact on career success and growth and the NQuotient founder is someone I knew from my days as a CDO (Chief Diversity Officer) at Cisco. I had developed a workshop that I delivered for the corporate sponsors of Watermark (the nonprofit I ran) around building meaningful connections and NQuotient was a great addition to the workshop and wanted to pilot with the Watermark community. I was leaving Watermark, and they asked if I'd join the team as a co-founder and officer. I have previously been at various times."

 118

What is most rewarding?

Marilyn enjoys helping others achieve their goals—something she now is able to do in multiple settings and on several levels.

What is most challenging?

This is an entrepreneurial position, so flexibility and resourcefulness are needed.

What about your MFT training is most helpful to you?

Marilyn comments, "I use systems thinking, how change affects systems, and respect for diversity in everything I do. I even use some of the concepts from short-term models, like the miracle question with some of my coaching clients who are stuck. In the workshop I do on unconscious bias, we talk extensively about systems and the impact on under-represented communities."

About diversity

Marilyn states, "I'm a 50-year-old Caucasian woman with a disability, I have a daughter who is a lesbian, my husband is Hispanic, and so I have personally experienced the challenges of diversity and inclusion."

JODI'S STORY

Jodi Prohofsky, Senior Director Channel Management,
Walmart Health and Wellness

Background

Jodi is a licensed MFT with a doctoral degree. She is currently the Senior Director of Channel Management at Walmart Health and Wellness.

What is this job like?

Jodi oversees a team of professionals and is "responsible for billions of dollars in provider contracts (Pharmacy, Optical, Immunizations, Medical, Durable Medical Equipment), which is part of a massive effort at Walmart to make healthcare more accessible and affordable." This brief description does not encompass the complexity of her work, which ultimately assists "millions of consumers who need more accessible and affordable options."

119

How do you get a job like this?

Jodi freely admits that the path towards corporate America was not in her plan. "If you has asked me back in 1992 if I would have spent the next 20+ years in Corporate America, I would have emphatically answered 'no.' I had no business acumen; at least that is what I thought.' However, Jodi found her career path taking an unexpected turn. She started working for an insurance company as a marriage and family therapist, while a doctoral student. Although she had planned on going into university-level teaching after graduation, she had an opportunity to go directly from graduation to work for the insurance company on the corporate level. Jodi held various positions in that company including Sr. VP of Clinical Operations, Head of Operations and Sr. VP of Clinical and Network Operations. Jodi shares that "I had grown up in the health insurance system and had what I considered a phenomenal career. But, I no longer felt that I could make a meaningful difference and therefore began to search for something new. I was working the usual trails on the common job search. One day I saw a small notice on LinkedIn about Walmart Health and Wellness. I posted a question to obtain more information . . . Within a few hours I had an outreach call from a recruiter who educated me about this large department in Walmart's Home Office and the work that was being done. She then informed me of an open position and I have to say I was intrigued."

What is most rewarding?

Jodi comments: "Being able to create change. Problem solving is key to this and I love a good problem. It now is very natural, but if I had to break it down and highlight how I apply my clinical training, it goes like this:

- Work to obtain an understanding from all key stakeholders on the definition of the business challenges or 'problem.'
- Assess if the problem is the same for everyone and who are the customers for change.
- Work through the story-finding reframes, helping others to define the solutions.
- Maintaining maneuverability in order to remove barriers to success is key to achieving the outcomes that are needed for a successful business model."

What is most challenging?

Jodi shares, "Change is always difficult—whether it is one person or an entire system. And, the bigger the system the harder it is to make change without going from 'ditch to ditch'." She also reflects about the complexities of her position.

"There is a lot of stress maneuvering through the multiple systems which at times may be moving in different directions."

What about your MFT training is most helpful to you?

Jodi had much to say on the influence of her MFT training on her work. "For me, one of the best parts of being a systemic thinker is that you know the ideas/solutions of today are good only for today—so you have to help the system to recognize that it will forever have to change in order to keep up with the changes of the world around it. So, never over-invest in a solution that is more than likely to change in the next year or two—invest wisely! By this I mean that I like to see solutions build onto themselves and allow the system to have enough flexibility to adapt to that change. In addition, you can't be afraid of 'throwaway' work—meaning that you may have to abandon the solution of today if it is no longer serving the system well." Jodi further reflects on her thinking about her systems training. "Regardless of the position title the focus truly boils down to leading people and processes in order to create change to improve the system." She says, "I realize and appreciate every day the value of my social and systemic education. In my opinion it has been more useful than a MBA would have been."

Finally, Jodi expands on details of her MFT education. "In order to innovate and keep the business relative there is a lot of mediation, maneuvering, and problem solving. My family therapy training taught me to interact with individuals in such a way that empowered them to solve their own problems by changing their frame of references. (Skills such as maintaining one's maneuverability, being one-down, listening, etc. were used, and still are, to determine how to find the mutually successful outcomes amongst business partners. The ability to understand problems, break solutions down into executable opportunities, and the tenacity to stay on task until the job got done led to exciting career and professional development opportunities."

About diversity

Jodi shares, "Everything about me, my family cultural background, my educational experience, my marital and family status, my gender identity, every experience is all part of my story. It is what shapes my world view. I learned a long time ago that I don't have to understand everyone's world view—it is actually an impossible task. Instead, I need to remember that it is an impossible task and therefore I should never assume I understand others' point of view. Instead, I need to remain curious and ask questions. It is also a personal imperative to remain my authentic self. I need to bring everything about me to every experience. For instance, when managing, developing, or mentoring others I am often asked to share my story about my career path. I am happy to do this. Every step of the way I learned something new. Every step of the way I made mistakes, continuously found ways to improve, tried new skills, and maintained my maneuverability. But, others can't take my path—they have to forge their own. So I listen to their story and then work with them to develop that path sometimes subtly and sometimes not so much— it all depends on them and how they need to process information in order to find and/or maintain their authentic self."

AVI'S STORY

Avi Lawrence, Entrepreneur, Therapy Product Inventor

Background

Avi is a licensed marriage and family therapist, who is also certified by the American College of Sports Medicine as an Exercise Physiologist. He currently works as Senior Therapist and Director of Recreation at Your Life Recovery Center in Boynton Beach Florida, an adult drug treatment facility, which provides the following levels of care: PHP, IOP, and outpatient services. With an entrepreneurial spirit, Avi has developed and produces an exercise system for children with ADHD and other diagnoses, called the Feelin Fit Bell.

What is this job like?

Avi comments, "Exercise turns on the attention system, the so-called executive functions—sequencing, working memory, prioritizing, inhibiting, and sustaining attention. On a practical level, it causes kids to be less impulsive, which makes them more primed to learn and develop self-confidence. Directly, a child with a higher level of self-confidence is less likely to bully or be bullied, improving the dynamic of the system this child interacts with as well." The Feelin Fit Bell system combines exercise and communication training, and involves the whole family. It is available for purchase at www.feelinfitbell.com.

How do you get a job like this?

Avi markets his tool online, and attends trade shows. He has tried out for the *Shark Tank* television show. He combines working on this product as an entrepreneur with his fulltime job in the field.

What is most rewarding?

Avi finds it rewarding to have developed a creative and novel approach, which is unique to him.

What is most challenging?

Paperwork at his "day job" and finding enough time to do it all are challenges he faces.

What about your MFT training is most helpful to you?

Avi notes, "The idea for Feelin Fit Bell came to me when studying marriage and family therapy. I wanted to utilize a component of a postmodern approach, to help engage children to express personal feelings without the focus on conceptualizing diagnosis and pathologizing responses and reactions. The Feelin Fit Bell system encourages all members within the 'family system' to engage in an 'inclusive activity' that promotes creativity and healthy relationships without infusing pathologies. Each participant provides 'creative input' with the focus on co-creating familial experiences." The tool is thus rooted in family therapy ideas.

About diversity

Avi notes, "I am a 44-year-old Caucasian male, ethnicity Jewish. I was raised with an appreciation for people from all cultures, races, and ethnicities. Within my own family I have members from the Middle East, Latin America, Eastern Europe, Canada, Australia, and the United Kingdom. I believe my rich ancestral diverse background provides me with the ability to empathetically connect and join with clients of various cultures and understand the various defining characteristics of a wide demographic of individuals. In addition, I can relate to individuals who have been racially oppressed and marginalized, as a third generation of Holocaust survivors myself. Both my maternal grandparents were in Auschwitz."

Chapter 15

About Equine-Assisted Family Therapy

Anne Rambo

Equine-assisted psychotherapy has grown exponentially in the past decade. This is therapy which integrates experiential activities with a horse into the therapy practice. There is a national certifying body, the Equine Assisted Growth and Learning Association (www.eagala.org), and at least one COAMFTE-accredited master's program, Nova Southeastern University, which offers a specialization in this modality. Other types of animal-assisted therapy practices may be utilized as well (as in therapy dogs and the use of pets). We interview a marriage and family therapist who became interested in this model and now does it full time.

OUR SUCCESS STORY RECOMMENDS ...

Talia's story captures the need for specialized training and experience in the area of equine-assisted therapy. She loves her job, and working with horses, which is critical.

TALIA'S STORY

Talia Aguayo, Therapist, Equine-Assisted Psychotherapy

Background

Talia is a licensed marriage and family therapist. She has completed additional training in Trauma-Focused Equine-Assisted Psychotherapy, and completed her portfolio for certification as a Mental Health Provider and Equine Specialist with the Equine Assisted Growth and Learning Association (EAGALA). She also has been trained in level 1 and 2 of the Trauma Resiliency Model (TRM). Talia works full time at an agency/stables that provides only equine-assisted therapy.

What is this job like?

The agency is a small one, so Talia wears multiple hats. She is Director of Operations, Lead Mental Health Provider, and Equine Specialist. She supervises other therapists; runs groups for veterans, children, team building, and other contracted purposes; she conducts individual couple and family sessions; and handles invoices. She also attends community events to publicize the program.

How do you get a job like this?

Talia fell in love with the agency when attending training held for the general mental health community. Fortunately the feeling was mutual! As she tells the story, "After my first training in 2012 I was in awe and knew this was it for me. This is what I had been looking for and I knew I had found what I was meant to do. It was like a breath of fresh air after feeling overwhelmed and burnt out in my previous private nonprofit agency job. In 2013 I attended an additional training at the farm, and at the end of the day I purchased a book written by the owner to get a better understanding on what equine-assisted therapy (EAP) was all about, how it worked, and what the business side looked like. I asked her to sign it for me, and she wrote, 'Welcome to the Herd.' I was not sure what she meant and asked. To my delight she told me that she liked me, saw potential in me, and that I would be a good fit for their staff. About a month later I was able to fill two part-time positions that became open. I handed in my resignation letter to the job that I had at the time and I have never looked back.

"It was scary to leave something that was comfortable and stable—not knowing if I would be able to financially live on what my heart and gut were telling me to do. With the support of my awesome boyfriend and amazing family, I took the jump and to this day I do not regret it!" Talia encourages all beginning therapists to stay open to trying new modalities and experiences.

What is most rewarding?

Talia bubbles with enthusiasm about this work. "Everything is rewarding! I love how I feel appreciated by my boss and fellow co-workers. I love my two-legged and four-legged co-workers. I love that every day is different. I love how that in one session you can get so much information from a client that they would not provide in months of therapy otherwise."

What is most challenging?

Once she took the plunge to try this new way of working, Talia has not encountered any major challenges to date. It seems like the perfect fit for her.

What about your MFT Training is most useful to you?

Talia credits systems thinking and having learned to respect the client as an expert. As she puts it, "I'm a sounding board, a safe place for clients to explore their options and create their own solutions."

About diversity

Talia feels she has learned to value and appreciate diversity. "Coming from Puerto Rico and moving to the States taught me about being more patient with others when they say ignorant or derogatory things about my culture. Instead of getting snappy, I educate. We are all different but the same and we need to celebrate and respect that. I try my hardest to not assume and ask questions when I am not sure. I believe this helps others, and myself, take ownership and be able to educate others. I believe we learn something new every day."

Chapter 16

About International Settings

Tommie V. Boyd

This book is designed primarily for the benefit of graduates of COAMFTE-accredited family therapy programs, in the United States. But just because someone graduates from one of these programs, does not mean he or she will necessarily stay in the United States. These degrees are well regarded internationally, and many graduates have attained success in other countries. We have comments from graduates in Jamaica, Iceland, Peru, and Taiwan.

OUR SUCCESS STORIES RECOMMEND . . .

Keep in touch with contacts in your home country (or the country you wish to make your home). Let them know about your education and your plans. Once relocated, be aware the mental health delivery system may be different, and you will need to accommodate accordingly. Hold on to what you have learned, however, and be confident in sharing these new ideas.

KAREN'S STORY

Karen Kinchin, Iceland

Karen has worked both in her native Iceland and in the United States since her graduation from a United States COAMFTE-accredited master's program. While in Iceland, "I worked with a nonprofit organization called Stigamot (http://www.stigamot.is/is/languages/english). It was perhaps the most valuable experience of all the valuable experiences I have had since graduating. It was a true grassroots organization, very political, feminist, and active. If we had not moved back to the US, I would still be there. My role was a therapist, teacher, presenter, fundraising person, etc. I met with individuals, families, and developed and conducted groups. I also dabbled in private practice, but because Iceland has socialized medicine, it was all out-of-pocket pay. I did work with an organization that dealt with

129

problematic gambling and conducted groups for them." Since returning to the States, she has developed an interest in private practice, as well as continuing her community-oriented work: "I organized a fundraiser similar to the 'Bag Ladies' project at the agency in south Florida."

DOREEN'S STORY

Doreen Blake, Jamaica

Doreen returned to Jamaica after graduation, after some time in the United States. She comments, "Immediately after graduation, I worked in South Florida for six years in both nonprofit and private agencies providing home-based therapy to at-risk youths and their families; My MFT training was utilized working with intact families, divorced families, and gay couples as well as substance abusers and domestic violence victims. I agree that when MFTs facilitate therapy in the home, we get to experience first-hand the family dynamics, the relational ethics, the fairness in the relationship, and how systems are inter-connected." After that time she returned to Jamaica, and adapted what she had learned. "What I experience here in Jamaica with regards to my qualifications is how to maneuver myself and how to creatively apply my profession. I do not need to be licensed here. Jamaica does not have that kind of criteria. I live in the Corporate area of the Capital of Jamaica—Kingston/St. Andrew. I have a few friends who are medical practitioners, and I get referral from them, and some 'word of mouth' by people who know me and what I do. I counsel children of associates who are not adjusting to adulthood, who are challenged with depression, panic attacks/anxiety, as well as children of the middle class who struggle with academic under-achievement, substance usage, and peer pressure. I charge anywhere between J$5,000 to J$8,000 (US $50–80) per session (one hour), sometimes even less. I conduct sessions at my home office and on occasion I will make home visits. Whenever any client comes to me it is usually very private. I do not refer to my sessions as 'therapy.' Here they think only 'mad people' go to therapy." So Doreen refers to herself as a counselor. Her practice is building and she is making a difference every day.

JONATHAN'S STORY

Jonathan Stiglich, Peru

Jonathan has gone back and forth between the United States and his native country of Peru since his graduation. He now works as an addictions therapist in the United States (in residential treatment settings). Jonathan found, "Even in Peru, being a marriage and family therapist was uncommon but appreciated. The psychiatrist I worked for was also a marriage and family therapist originally, or as they called it in Peru *sistemico*, which means systemic. Those who did practice systemic therapy only knew the structural model. I stayed in Peru for a year, working two jobs in Lima, the capital; one was with a Jesuit private school as an upper school therapist and the other was working for a well-known psychiatrist in Miraflores, bordering San Isidro. Both districts consist of mostly the upper classes." Since his return to the States, Jonathan has worked in substance abuse treatment. He comments on some good advice he received that has been beneficial in both countries and all settings: "If you want to be a good therapist you have to take a page out of the samurai philosophy: You have to experience life not just with your sword in the battlefield but learning things that have nothing to do with what you do for a living—the key here is building perspective and creativity. One of the things I was taught by an MFT professor was to 'stay curious.' This has always stuck with me; if you are curious you ask great questions as opposed to basic ones. Our core philosophy is that we aren't experts in our clients' lives but we are experts at asking questions."

PEI-FEN'S STORY

Pei-Fen Li, Taiwan

Pei Fen obtained her master's degree in family therapy from the University of Oregon. She then returned to Taiwan to work as a guidance counselor, thus fulfilling her job contract with the Taiwanese government. She notes, "The principal, colleagues, and students' parents valued my education background and clinical experiences in the US. I was also recruited to do a part-time counseling job at the Kaohsiung Student Counseling Center, where schools referred their most challenging cases to the center for therapy. I visited students' school and their home, talked to their parents and assisted their teachers to understand students' issues. During the second year of my re-entry, I was appointed to be a clinical group leader in the school and started to involve administration work." She found she had to make some adaptations to the Taiwanese context. "The most rewarding part for me was to see growth and change my students and their families had gone through. I noticed that people in Taiwan valued my professional opinions much and often called me 'teacher,' not 'therapist' or my name. I shifted my clinical model to correspond to clients' needs and expectations. The most challenging part was to adjust the ethics I had learned from the US and to figure out alternative ways to fit local cultures. For example, I once needed to make a mandatory report about a sexual abuse case in the school. As a group leader, I needed to assist the principal and the administrative supervisor to form an investigation group. I also arranged counseling services for students and contacted students' parents. As a guidance teacher who was professionally trained in the field, I was expected by colleagues to continue dialogues with students throughout the investigation process. I was performing multiple roles at one time and finally experienced burnout myself. The principal and my supervisor trusted my knowledge and professional judgments and needed my involvement, but I felt overwhelmed and did not feel supported. I later decided to leave the school and came back to the US to pursue a PhD degree." Pei-Fen feels her MFT training gave her valuable clinical skills. "However, it did not mean what I had learned in the US was always applicable. In fact, I needed to make adaption oftentimes, or even challenge myself. Sometimes, I did not have an answer and needed to figure out by myself. Sometimes, discussions with my colleagues could help. I did not join professional supervision then and wish that I could do so if I encountered the situation again." She has advice for others who plan to work internationally. "Be willing to unlearn what you have known and to learn what you don't know. People in different cultures perceive psychotherapy differently. For some cultures, pursuing psychotherapy is not a common option. Clinicians need to creatively develop ways to meet clients' needs and deliver culturally relevant interventions to address clients' issues. Seeing clients in the office might not work and clinicians may need to step out of their comfort zone to visit where clients are. Discussing some Western cultural values (e.g., leaving home as being independent) might not make sense to clients; clinicians should be aware of local cultural values and modify professional judgments in delivering interventions."

Chapter 17

And in Conclusion . . .

Anne Rambo, Tommie V. Boyd, and
Martha Gonzalez Marquez

As we read through these "success stories," certain themes emerge which may be useful to those contemplating careers in marriage and family therapy. We notice that:

1   Nearly all of our successful examples began their careers working for private nonprofit agencies, often with at-risk youth and indigent families. This important work is great training as well as socially responsible. Even if one plans on private practice or managed care or another type of setting, getting some pre-licensure experience with a private nonprofit seems like a common and useful strategy.
2   Those who did go straight into private practice or into coaching allowed themselves time to build up a clientele, and offered free workshops and other events to stimulate interest in the community.
3   Marriage and family therapy skills are applicable in a wide variety of settings, including corporate and organizational settings. It seems to be useful to focus on one's skill set, rather than feel limited as to setting. Opportunities in all these areas will only increase over time, as the unique skills of marriage and family therapists become better known.
4   Thinking systemically and relationally was mentioned by virtually all of our success examples as the most useful part of their family therapy training. Specific brief therapy skills, and an appreciation of diversity, were also often cited.
5   Speaking of diversity, our success examples demonstrate how a wide range of personal experiences and contextual variables can enrich and deepen a therapist's skills. Many also noted the diverse populations they are fortunate to work with.

Many of our success stories cited the importance of extra training and/or education in specialized areas in order to be prepared to work with a particular population or in a particular setting. This will also set one apart from other competing professionals in the area.

The importance of excellent supervision not only in one's training but also throughout one's practice was also highlighted. Our field has finally reached a place of maturity to have seasoned mentors and supervisors who are ready and excited to pass on their wisdom and experience. These mentors are systemically and relationally trained to assist new therapists to navigate the multitude of settings in which they can work.

Our success stories also demonstrate the value of openness and curiosity. So many shared how they often planned on one route for their professional career but found opportunities and passion in another direction. The relationship with peers and other professionals has opened doors for many of these therapists to pursue work in previously unknown areas.

Index

Aguayo, Talia (equine-assisted psychotherapy therapist) 125–7

Akhturallah, Shazia (supervisor for managed care agency) 85–7

Alenazi, Amnah (marital educator in mosque settings) 106–8

American Association of Marital and Family Therapy Regulatory Board 5

American Association of Marriage and Family Therapy (AAMFT) 8, 47, 71, 112

Apache Behavioral Health Services, Inc. (ABHS) 111, 112

attachment theory 3

Azulay, Gabrielle (matchmaker/coach) 63–5

Bateson, Gregory 3, 4

Blake, Doreen 130

Bowen, Murray 3

Bowen Theory 33

Boys and Girls Clubs of America (BGCA) 110

Braeger, Jacqueline (Jacquie) (Assistant Professor) 96–8

Carbone, Holly 111–13

challenges of working as a marriage and family therapist: coaching 63, 64, 66, 68; collaboration with other professions 56–7, 58–9; corporate and entrepreneurial work 119, 120–1, 123; equine-assisted family therapy 126; faith-based settings 101, 102, 103–4, 105, 107; higher education (university and postgraduate) settings 92, 94–5, 97; Indian related health services/similar settings 111, 112, 115; managed care 84–5, 86–7, 89; military settings 73, 75, 77–8, 79, 82; private nonprofit agencies 15, 18, 19, 21, 22–3; private practice settings 37, 40, 42, 43–4, 46; residential treatment settings 27, 29, 30, 33; school-based settings 49, 50, 52, 53

Christian COOPS of America 101

coaching 61–9; story of Alex 62–3; story of Gaby 63–5; story of Katia 65–6; story of Trish 67–9

COAMFTE see Commission on Accreditation in Marital and Family Therapy Education (COAMFTE), US

collaboration with other professions 55–9; story of Brian 56–7; story of Randy 57–9

Commission on Accreditation in Marital and Family Therapy Education (COAMFTE), US 1, 4, 6, 14, 71, 129

corporate and entrepreneurial work 117–23; story of Avi 122–3; story of Jodi 119–22; story of Marilyn 118–19
Corrington, Samantha (registered counselor) 113–16
couples therapy 3
Crist, Elissa (clinical specialist in Marine Corps) 76–8
cybernetics 3

Dental Assistance Services for Survivors of the Holocaust (DASH) 100
diversity considerations 7; coaching 63, 64–5, 66, 68–9; collaboration with other professions 57, 59; corporate and entrepreneurial work 119, 121–2, 123; equine-assisted family therapy 127; faith-based settings 101, 102–3, 104, 106, 107–8; higher education (university and postgraduate) settings 93, 95, 98; Indian related health services/similar settings 111, 113, 116; managed care 85, 87, 89–90; military settings 73–4, 76, 78, 80, 82; private nonprofit agencies 16, 18, 20, 21, 23; private practice settings 38, 41, 42, 44, 46; residential treatment settings 27–8, 29, 31, 33; school-based settings 49, 51, 52, 54
driving under the influence (DUI) 26

entrepreneurial work see corporate and entrepreneurial work
equine-assisted family therapy 125–7
Equine Assisted Growth and Learning Association (EAGALA) 125

faith-based settings 99–108; story of Amnah 106–8; story of Bobbi 104–6; story of Leslie 101–3; story of Pattie 100–1; story of Simone 103–4
family therapy 4; equine-assisted 125–7; gender and marriage 8–9
Faure, Julien 41–2

Federal Indian Health Services 109
federal loan programs 5
Finnis, Simone (former director of Protestant family ministry) 103–4
Foucault, Michel 4

Gales, Laura (marriage and family therapist for veterans) 74–6
Ganci, Philip (school-based family therapist) 48–9
gender, and marriage and family therapy 8–9
Genogram 33
Georgia Association for Marriage and Family Therapy (GAMFT) 43
Gershonov, Alina (intern) 36–8
globalization 9
Granie, Bryan (Assistant Director) 110–11
Griffin, Leslie (Protestant family life educator) 101–3
Guerin, Jamie (substance abuse therapist) 26–8
Gutierrez, Fabiola (Clinical Supervisor) 17–18

Heller, Randy (collaborative family law specialist) 57–9
higher education (university and postgraduate) settings 91–8
Hill, Tequilla 42–4
Howard, Walter (school-based family therapist) 49–51

inclusivity in marriage and family therapy 7–10; diversity and inclusivity in marriage and family therapy 7; and gender 8–9
Indian related health services/similar settings 5, 109–16; story of Bryan 110–11; story of Holly 111–13; story of Samantha 113–16
Individual Education Plans (IEPs) 48
Inner Therapeutic Solutions, LLC 36

international settings 129–32
interns 36–8, 39

Jayatilleke, Farheen (elementary school teacher) 53–4
Jewish Family Services 100
Jones, Alex (dating/relationship coach) 62–3

Kaohsiung Student Counseling Center, Taiwan 131
Kinchin, Karen 129–30
Knowledge Age 9
Koenig, Rosario (academic advisor) 92–3

LaFavor, Trahern (evidence-based program clinical supervisor) 19–20
Lawrence, Avi (entrepreneur) 122–3
Lemieux, Katie (trainer and supervisor) 44–6
LGBTQ clients 9, 27
Li, Pei-Fen 131–2; see also marriage and family therapy
licensure 13, 14, 109
loan programs 5

male therapists 8
managed care 83–90; story of Anne-Marie 84–5; story of Fariha 88–90; story of Shazia 85–7
Manfre, Anthony (marriage and family therapist for veterans) 72–4
Manns, Alonso 38–41
marriage and family therapists (MFTs) 1–34; aging of 7; becoming a high quality MFT 5–6; becoming an MFT 4–5; challenging aspects of job see challenges of working as a marriage and family therapist; and diversity see diversity considerations; global reach, working across and within borders 9–10; helpful aspects of training see training as a marriage and family therapist, helpful aspects; interview

subjects 1; nature of job see nature of work of marriage and family therapists (MFTs); obtaining a job see obtaining work as a marriage and family therapist; rewards see rewards of working as a marriage and family therapist; unique nature of marriage and family therapy 1–2; work of 2–4
military settings 71–82; story of Anthony 72–4; story of Elissa 76–8; story of Laura 74–6; story of Michele 81–2; story of Ronella 78–80
Mittal, M. 9
Modern Family Therapeutic Solutions LLC 36
multiple realities 3

Nagel, Marilyn (corporate co-founder consultant) 118–19
narrative therapy 4
National Association for Career Development 61
National Council on Family Relations 61
National Health Service Corps 5, 109
natural systems theory 3
nature of work of marriage and family therapists (MFTs): coaching 62, 63, 65, 67; collaboration with other professions 56, 58; corporate and entrepreneurial work 118, 119, 122; equine-assisted family therapy 126; faith-based settings 100, 101, 103, 104–5, 106; higher education (university and postgraduate) settings 92, 94, 96; Indian related health services/similar settings 110, 111, 114; managed care 84, 85–6, 88; military settings 72, 74, 76–7, 78–9, 81; private nonprofit agencies 14–15, 17, 19, 20, 22; private practice settings 36, 39, 41, 42–3, 45; residential treatment settings 26, 28, 30, 31–2; school-based settings 48, 50, 51, 53

Niazi, Fariha (training manager) 88–90
nonpathologizing, circular causality 3
nonprofit agencies, private 13–23; as
    common setting for entry-level
    positions in marriage and family
    therapy 13; Family Skill Builders
    program 17; story of Andrea 14–16;
    story of Fabiola 17–18; story of Liz
    22–3; story of Neolita 20–1; story of
    Trahern 19–20

object relations theory 3
obtaining work as a marriage and family
    therapist: and becoming a marriage
    and family therapist 4–5; coaching 62,
    64, 65, 67–8; collaboration with
    other professions 56, 58; corporate
    and entrepreneurial work 118, 120,
    122; equine-assisted family therapy
    126; faith-based settings 100, 102,
    103, 105, 107; higher education
    (university and postgraduate) settings
    92, 94, 96; Indian related health
    services/similar settings 110, 112,
    114–15; managed care 84, 86, 88;
    military settings 72–3, 75, 77, 79, 81;
    private nonprofit agencies 15, 17,
    19, 20–1, 22; private practice settings
    36–7, 39–40, 41, 43, 45; residential
    treatment settings 26, 28, 30, 32;
    school-based settings 48, 50, 51,
    53
O'Hanlon, Bill 5

Palmer, Lisa (eating disorders therapist)
    29–31
Peck Lauderdale, Susan (alternative
    school family therapist) 51–2
private practice settings 35–46; story of
    Adit and Alina 36–8; story of Alonso
    38–41; story of Julien 41–2; story of
    Katie 44–6; story of Tequilla 42–4
Prohofsky, Jodi (senior director channel
    management) 119–22

Renew Center (center for treatment of
    eating disorders) 29
residential treatment settings 25–33;
    Certified Addictions Professional
    designation 25; story of Jamie 26–8;
    story of Lisa 29–31; story of Nancy
    28–9; story of Sara 31–3
rewards of working as a marriage and
    family therapist: coaching 63, 64, 66,
    68; collaboration with other
    professions 56, 58; corporate and
    entrepreneurial work 119, 120, 122;
    equine-assisted family therapy 126;
    faith-based settings 100, 102, 103,
    105, 107; higher education (university
    and postgraduate) settings 92, 94,
    97; Indian related health
    services/similar settings 110, 112,
    115; managed care 84, 86, 88;
    military settings 73, 75, 77, 79, 81–2;
    private nonprofit agencies 15, 18, 19,
    21, 22; private practice settings 37,
    40, 41, 43, 45; residential treatment
    settings 26, 28, 30, 32; school-based
    settings 48, 50, 52, 53
Roedwald, Anne-Marie (intensive
    behavioral health case manager) 84–5
Rosenberg, Brian (Corporate Director)
    56–7

Schneider, Andrea (entry level agency
    therapist) 14–16
school-based settings 47–54; story of
    Farheen 53–4; story of Philip 48–9;
    story of Susy 51–2; story of Walter
    49–51; teaching certificates, value of
    47
Sharoni, Idit (intern) 36–8
Shulman, Liz (clinical consultant in
    interagency collaboration) 22–3
Sinkoe, Pattie (Director of Behavioral
    Health) 100–1
Smith, Sara (behavioral health residential
    homeless shelter supervisor) 31–3

138

Spitzer, Nancy (substance abuse therapist) 28–9
Stiglich, Jonathan 130–1
success stories: coaching 62–9; collaboration with other professions 55–9; corporate and entrepreneurial work 117–23; equine-assisted family therapy 125–7; faith-based settings 99–108; higher education (university and postgraduate) settings 91–8; Indian related health services/similar settings 109–16; international settings 129–32; managed care 83–90; military settings 71–82; nonprofit agencies, private 14–23; private practice settings 35–46; residential treatment settings 26–33; school-based settings 47–54
systems theory 3

Tikhonravova, Katia (sales coach) 65–6
training as a marriage and family therapist, helpful aspects: coaching 63, 64, 66, 68; collaboration with other professions 57, 59; corporate and entrepreneurial work 121, 123;

equine-assisted family therapy 127; faith based settings 101, 102, 104, 105–6, 107; higher education (university and postgraduate) settings 93, 95, 97; Indian related health services/similar settings 111, 113, 115; managed care 85, 87, 89; military settings 73, 75–6, 78, 80, 82; private nonprofit agencies 16, 18, 20, 21, 23; private practice settings 37–8, 40–1, 42, 44, 46; residential treatment settings 27, 29, 30, 33; school-based settings 49, 50–1, 52, 54
Trauma Resiliency Model (TRM) 125
Turner, Patricia (career coach) 67–9

Vetenary Centers 71
Veterans Administration 71
Von Bertanlanffy, Ludwig 3

Walter, Ili maris Rivera (adjunct instructor) 93–5
Weiner, Norbert 3
Wieling, E. 9

yoga 36–7

Taylor & Francis eBooks

Helping you to choose the right eBooks for your Library

Add Routledge titles to your library's digital collection today. Taylor and Francis ebooks contains over 50,000 titles in the Humanities, Social Sciences, Behavioural Sciences, Built Environment and Law.

Choose from a range of subject packages or create your own!

Benefits for you

» Free MARC records
» COUNTER-compliant usage statistics
» Flexible purchase and pricing options
» All titles DRM-free.

Benefits for your user

» Off-site, anytime access via Athens or referring URL
» Print or copy pages or chapters
» Full content search
» Bookmark, highlight and annotate text
» Access to thousands of pages of quality research at the click of a button.

REQUEST YOUR **FREE** INSTITUTIONAL TRIAL TODAY

Free Trials Available
We offer free trials to qualifying academic, corporate and government customers.

eCollections – Choose from over 30 subject eCollections, including:

Archaeology	Language Learning
Architecture	Law
Asian Studies	Literature
Business & Management	Media & Communication
Classical Studies	Middle East Studies
Construction	Music
Creative & Media Arts	Philosophy
Criminology & Criminal Justice	Planning
Economics	Politics
Education	Psychology & Mental Health
Energy	Religion
Engineering	Security
English Language & Linguistics	Social Work
Environment & Sustainability	Sociology
Geography	Sport
Health Studies	Theatre & Performance
History	Tourism, Hospitality & Events

For more information, pricing enquiries or to order a free trial, please contact your local sales team: www.tandfebooks.com/page/sales

 Routledge Taylor & Francis Group

The home of Routledge books

www.tandfebooks.com